To Will,
Happy Birthday 1997!
I do remember some good
times, do you?

Love,
Cheryl

THE
VILLA D'ESTE
AT TIVOLI

Oval Fountain detail

THE
VILLA D'ESTE
AT TIVOLI

DAVID DERNIE

Photographs by Alastair Carew-Cox

AD ACADEMY EDITIONS

ACKNOWLEDGEMENTS

The author wishes to thank, above all, Anna Reali whose help, guidance, knowledge of the culture and translations from Italian were invaluable. Grateful thanks also to Dalibor Vesely whose teaching and inspiration is the foundation of this work, and to Peter Carl who first suggested the project and whose help and encouragement sustained it.

This research was undertaken during two years' Scholarship at the British School at Rome. The author remains indebted to the School, to the support of Richard Hodges (then Director), the excellent library, Valerie Scott, Beatrice Gelosia, Rita Petrollini, Simona Fioranelli, and to all the staff, particularly Maria Pia Malvezzi.

Grateful thanks are extended to Loredana Alibrandi and to the Soprintendza per i Beni Ambientali e Architettonici del Lazio for their kind permission to publish the photographs, and to the staff of the Villa d'Este, its Director Isabella Barisi, and Francesco Caretta for his expert guidance. Thanks also to Michael Foster for his interpretation of biblical themes (especially the courtyard entrance), to Deborah Howard for her advice, to Alioune Sow for his translations from French, to Robert Gassner for his translations from Latin.

Further thanks are extended by David Dernie and Alastair Carew-Cox to ICL (Individual Colour Laboratories Ltd) and Fuji Photo Film (UK) Ltd for their valuable assistance in this project. The photographs were taken using Fuji professional film and were hand-printed by ICL photographic laboratories on Fuji professional paper. Thanks to Mary Stamos and John Cohen at Fuji, and John Azmat, Simon Ward, Marie Bayliss and Alison Henry at ICL.

We would also particularly like to thank the trustees of The Interbuild Fund for their enthusiastic support.

We are also grateful to The Building Centre Trust and The Kathleen and Margery Elliott Scholarship Trust for helping to fund this project. Thanks also to the staff at Academy, to Maggie Toy, Andrea Bettella, and especially to Lucy Ryan for editing the text and Gregory Mills for designing the layout.

A special thanks from Alastair to Debra whose support and understanding helped to make this work possible.

Illustration credits: p25, Pirro Ligorio, *Design for the Illusionist, decoration of an interior wall*, cat no JBS 516, courtesy The Governing Body, Christ Church, Oxford; p25, Pirro Ligorio, *panel of decoration in the Grotesque style*, neg no P1149, courtesy The Ashmolean Museum, Oxford; p26, Du Pérac, *Villa d'Este, 1572*, accession no 41.72(3), neg no MM24259, courtesy The Metropolitan Museum of Art, New York; p26, courtesy The Metropolitan Museum of Art, New York, Harris Brisbane Dick Fund, 1941 (41, 72, (3)); pp45, 50, 82, 91, 95, Vincenzo Cartari, *Le Imagini degli Dei*, shelfmark: Douce.C.306, courtesy The Bodleian Library, Oxford; p29, Pirro Ligorio, *The Dance of Salome*, inv no 1964-3-31-1, courtesy The British Museum, London.

COVER: Water Organ, Grottoes of the Tiburtine Sibyl and Neptune

First published in Great Britain in 1996 by
ACADEMY EDITIONS
An imprint of

ACADEMY GROUP LTD
42 Leinster Gardens, London W2 3AN
Member of the VCH Publishing Group

ISBN 1 85490 447 7

Distributed to the trade in the United States of America by
NATIONAL BOOK NETWORK, INC
4720 Boston Way, Lanham, Maryland 20706

Printed and bound in the UK

CONTENTS

Preface   6

Introduction   8

Ligorio's Tiburtine Antiquities   20

The Fountain of the Dragon: Jupiter's Crystal Cave   34

The Fountain of Neptune and the Lower Garden   46

The Tiburtine Sibyl   54

The Water Organ   62

The Oval Fountain   72

The Grotto of Venus and the Fountains of Bacchus   82

The Fountain of the Owls   84

The Rometta   88

The Grotto of Diana   94

The Salotto   104

The Line of a Hundred Fountains: Apotheosis at the End of Time   114

Notes   124

Selected Bibliography   128

Line of a Hundred Fountains

Preface

The Villa d'Este is one of the most visited and well-known monuments in Italy, but in terms of the definition of key elements of its iconography, it is still a mystery. The difficulty arises from the general lack of documentation, the contradictory nature of that which does exist and, in my opinion, the discrepancy between original intention and the garden as it appears today. A few years ago the Comitato Nazionale Ligoriano began a further study of documentary information, including Pirro Ligorio's *Libri delle Antichità*, which could in future deepen our thematic understanding and open up new roads of investigation. However, to date there have been only a few interpretations of the symbolic content of the garden. Of these, David Coffin was the first to discuss the themes relating to Tivoli and Rome, those involving Hercules, to whom Muret dedicates the garden, and the Tiburtine Sibyl, suggesting that these mythological subjects could be given a Christian interpretation. More recently, Maria Luisa Madonna has written several articles illuminating further the relationship between the garden, the Tiburtine Sibyl, the Tiburtine landscape and Rome.

David Dernie's research carries forward the hypothesis identified by Coffin, offering a completely new interpretation of the iconography of the garden. His work provides answers to questions which have troubled even those who, like myself, have known the garden for many years. It is, for example, impossible not to notice that the articulation of the plan, as a series of orthogonal axes, is contradicted by the spatial perception of the garden. The actual garden is more varied and complex, experienced more as a rhythm of journeys, and Dernie manages to reformulate the hidden meaning of these passages.

To date, publications on the Villa d'Este have largely ignored a formal relationship with the surrounding landscape, treating the garden as a microcosm, closed within itself. In reality, no visitor can fail to observe that, at least on a visual level, a strong link with the Tiburtine landscape was intended. Dernie is the first to explore this relationship: linking the villa with the principal archaeological sites still present in the surrounding urban fabric, he illustrates that these orientations determined the location of the fountains within the grid of the garden's layout.

As curator of the garden, I am fascinated by this fresh way of seeing and interpreting, as explained by Dernie. At the same time, I am convinced that this renewed interest in the Villa d'Este could result in new insights, particularly in light of the recent discovery in the villa of enigmatic drawings and writings relating to two of the garden's key symbols: the dragon and the oval, which are published here for the first time.

Isabella Barisi
Director of the Villa d'Este

THE
VILLA D'ESTE
AT TIVOLI

Introduction

'The pen cannot depict it. The first sight does not provide a full comprehension of the matter: only long enduring consideration of its particular parts lets admiration rise by degrees.'

Umberto Foglietta, 1569

The Villa d'Este, created under Cardinal Ippolito d'Este of Ferrara between 1550-72, is perhaps the most spectacular garden in the whole of Italy. Poetic and literary descriptions, paintings, and in particular the well-known engraving by the French architect Etienne Du Pérac, assured the garden's popularity throughout Europe until well into the seventeenth century, when the garden itself was poorly maintained and the royal garden at Versailles began to draw attention. Representing the humanist culture of one of Europe's most powerful nobles, it is now carefully tended and remains largely intact, as a striking reminder of the particular fascination that the domain of the garden held for late sixteenth-century culture.

Despite the enormous scale and expense of the project, the Cardinal spent only two or three summer months at the villa, and then only for a few years.[1] Son of Alphonso I and Lucrezia Borgia, he was made governor of Tivoli as a result of the papal enclave which gathered in 1549 following the death of Pope Paul III. The post was a political reward for his direct support of the bid of Giovan Maria Cardinal del Monte to become Pope Julius III. Tivoli was an ancient rival of Rome, lying some seventeen miles to the east, and was rich in antique ruins of numerous and important Roman villas and temples, among them the temples to Hercules Victor and Hercules Saxanus, the villas of the Emperor Hadrian and Quintillius Varus, and the well-known circular temple of the Tiburtine Sibyl. There the Cardinal established one of Italy's most erudite courts which, whilst perhaps not competing with the refinement of Florence, was certainly to challenge the Medici court with its innovation.

The Cardinal engaged at his court well-established artists such as Girolamo Muziano, Federico Zuccaro and Benvenuto Cellini, the musician Nicola Vicentino, the humanists Marc-Antoine Muret, Francesco Bandini Piccolomini and Umberto Foglietta, and the Neapolitan antiquarian Pirro Ligorio (1513/14-84). Ligorio accompanied the Cardinal during his first visit to the region and set about a large number of excavations, including one of Hadrian's Villa. His vast *opus*, the *Libri delle Antichità*, which consists of some thirty-nine manuscript volumes (now in the archives of Naples and Turin), gives an infinitely detailed account of the geographical, historical, mythological and legendary background of an enormous range of topics, from rivers and fountains to dress and manners. Had it been published, Ligorio's fame would certainly have rivalled that of his great adversary, Giorgio Vasari (1511-74).

Some of the statuary found during these early excavations was re-used at the Villa d'Este – the Cardinal was a keen collector – but there is an altogether more important outcome of Ligorio's involvement at this stage, for so much of the character and topographic layout of the garden depended on his immense knowledge of local and classical legends and history. Ligorio is widely acknowledged as the architect of the Villa d'Este, and although in the building records of 1549-55 he is referred to as an *antiquarian*, this should not be taken literally. It would be a mistake to underestimate his role during this period in conceiving the complex iconographic programme for the garden.[2]

With Ligorio as his close advisor, the Cardinal began to purchase land in the vicinity of the Franciscan monastery attached to Santa Maria Maggiore, part of which was traditionally rented to the ecclesiastical governors of Tivoli. The medieval cloister overlooked the Valle Gaudente, whose steep, west-facing slopes were to be transformed into the terraces of the Villa d'Este gardens. The Cardinal was to rebuild the courtyard, substantially extend the residence facing the garden, and demolish a large section of the old town, including several churches, retaining only the old defensive wall to define the western boundary of the garden.

A much-noted characteristic of Ligorio's texts is his emphasis on historical, mythical and legendary context, and his undoubted involvement with the Estense court at Tivoli during the conception of the villa suggests that the meaning of the garden was also carefully interwoven with Tiburtine legend and with the ancient past buried in its landscape of ruins. It is not a coincidence that the principal Roman cults of the Tiburtine region – the Emperors, Hercules, Augustales, Juno, Jupiter, Diana, Bona Dea, Mars, Neptunus Adiutor, Venus Obsequens and Aesculapius – are all important to the iconography of the garden.[3] These pagan gods were symbols of Tivoli's golden past, and their temples were the very foundation stones of a regeneration of the Catholic church that was pursued with a determination characteristic of the Counter

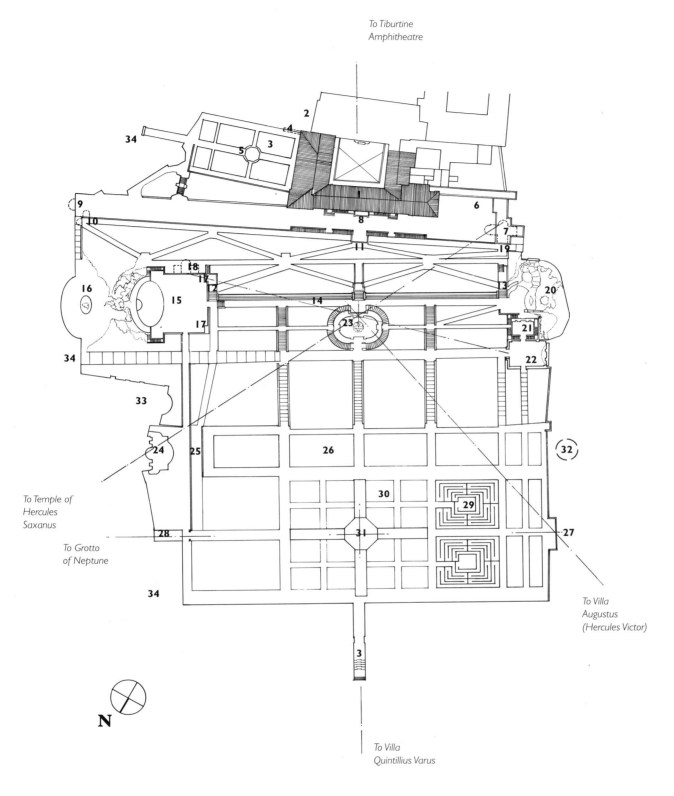

To Tiburtine
Amphitheatre

To Temple of
Hercules
Saxanus

To Grotto
of Neptune

To Villa
Augustus
(Hercules Victor)

N

To Villa
Quintillius Varus

ABOVE: Plan, partial reconstruction, drawing by David Dernie based on a survey by the Soprintendenza per i Beni Ambientali e Architettonici del Lazio (1) villa (2) entrance to courtyard (3) main entrance to garden, Viale della Prospettiva (4) Fountain of the Unicorn (5) pavilion (6) tennis court (7) dining loggia (8) Fountain of Leda (9) Fountain of Thetis (10) Fountain of Aesculapius and Hygieia (11) Fountain of Pandora (12) Fountain of Pomona (13) Fountain of Flora (14) Line of a Hundred Fountains (15) Oval Fountain (16) Fountain of Pegasus (17) Fountains of Bacchus (18) Grotto of Venus (19) Grotto of Diana (20) Fountain of Rome (21) Fountain of the Emperors (22) Fountain of the Owls (23) Fountain of the Dragon (24) Water Organ (25) Grottoes of the Sibyl (26) fish pools (27) Fountain of Neptune, author's interpretation (28) Fountain of Venus Cloacina (29) labyrinths (30) herb gardens (31) octagonal pavilion (32) position of Neptune Fountain according to Du Pérac (33) Church of S Pietro della Carità (34) secondary entrances; OVERLEAF: View from the north from Villa Quintillius Varus. To the left is the tower on the site of the Temple of Hercules Saxanus; directly behind the Villa d'Este is the top edge of the Rocca Pia (on the edge of the Tiburtine amphitheatre) and to the right is the Temple of Hercules Victor (which Ligorio interprets as Villa Augustus)

Reformation, redoubled after the termination of the Council of Trent in 1563.

From 1555 to 1563, however, little work was carried out on the villa. With the election of Pope Paul IV in 1555, the Cardinal was removed from the governorship of Tivoli and banished to Lombardy. And although Pius IV restored the Cardinal to the governorship in 1560, he subsequently sent him to serve as Papal Legate to France. During these difficult years, Ligorio was architect to Pius IV. His main contribution lay in his design of the Casino in the Vatican gardens, but he spent a short time in jail, standing accused of wishing to change Michelangelo's plans for St Peter's. He returned to the service of the Cardinal between 1567 and 1569 to design two of the garden's principal fountains, the Rometta and the Oval Fountain, which rework some of the themes portrayed in the stucco decoration of the Vatican Casino. By this stage, most of the major engineering works required to raise the level of the lowest part of the valley had been completed. Work was also underway on the two-storey loggia on the northwest facade. The hydraulic system was in the hands of Curzio Maccerone, who started work in 1566 after completing the fountains at the Cardinal's Rome residence on Monte Cavallo. The main water source for the garden was the River Aniene channelled underneath the town itself, whilst a second source came from a stream called the Rivellese in the distant hills of S Angelo. Maccerone developed a system which separated these two water sources, so that the Aniene fed the fountains to the north while the Rivellese, whose water was renowned for its purity, was reserved for the fountains in the upper parts of the garden. In coordinating the water supply in this way, Maccerone was no doubt working closely with Ligorio, whose conception of the garden's fountains involved an intricate symbolism in which water represented a mysterious creative spirit of the natural world. Maccerone's hydraulic system was to represent the divinely ordained natural cycle of water between sky and ocean.

Ligorio was a brilliant draughtsman,[4] modelling his style after Polidoro da Caravaggio and Michelangelo. His drawings, however, were rarely concerned with the issue of *maniera*, with style itself, but were precisely attuned to the allegorical content of each figural composition. Rarely, for instance, did he concentrate on colour, tone and imitation of material in his drawn and painted works – a constant preoccupation of Mannerist painters from Perin del Vaga to Salviati. Instead, his invariably monotone drawings focused the issue of figural gesture and detail of composition. Vastly erudite in many fields, Ligorio, like Vitruvius, stated that an architect should be:

> knowledgeable and practical [and] it is best to learn philosophy, musical method, geometry [. . .], mathematics, astronomy, history, morality, medicine, geography, cosmography, topography, analogy, perspective, sculpture, painting, and to demonstrate varied inventions.[5]

It was this encyclopaedic erudition which gave rise to the deeply layered and elusive allegories that characterise the architecture of the Villa d'Este and its gardens.

This is an architecture which owes much to Raphael, and in particular to the Villa Madama built for Cardinal Giuliano de' Medici (Clement VII) on the slopes of Monte Mario in Rome. Designed shortly before Raphael's death in 1520, and remaining incomplete because of the Sack of Rome in 1527, the villa represents an important shift in the development of the late-Renaissance garden. In contrast, for example, to Bramante's design for the terraced Belvedere Court (1504-c1513) for Julius II, the sequence of interpenetrating garden spaces is not structured as a single perspective. Rather, the Villa Madama is a cluster of settings, an altogether more complex sequence whose constant reference is the permanence and continuity of the dark hillside itself.[6]

The Cardinal rented the Villa Madama from Catherine de' Medici during the papal enclave of 1549, so it is perhaps not surprising that the radically fragmented typography of the Villa d'Este gardens (more akin to the distorted compositions of a Mannerist painting than to the geometrical order of the early-Renaissance garden) should have grown out of the shift in understanding achieved by Raphael several decades earlier. Both Raphael and Ligorio engaged the topography of the hillside, which is first represented in primary orientations of architectural elements such as double walls, fountain niches and deep fish pools. This garden architecture is characterised by a play of shadow (rather than light) which seeks to imbue some of the mystery of the earth's darkness into the architectural setting itself. Nature is understood as constantly changing, metamorphic, a *Natura Generante*, and the architecture reaches out to capture its creative *anima*.

The chance discovery of Nero's *Domus Aurea* at the end of the fifteenth century provided an impulse for artists to develop the antique style of Grotesque decoration, a language which in the following century expressed the growing fascination with rendering the very creativity of the earth, to reveal God's presence hidden in its darkness. Filippo Lippi, Pinturicchio and Signorelli were among the first to introduce this style into the sixteenth century, and the loggia in the Vatican (1517-19) by Raphael and Giovanni da Udine became a touchstone for its further development. These Grotesque figures, full of deft brush strokes and inventive colour combinations, create a rhythm of transformational creatures, often half-formed and half-deformed at the same time. There is a fascination with a world of invented species which appear to float weightlessly on an otherwise blank surface. Fantastical creatures combine animal with plant, real with mythical, to create an unreal world pointing to a hidden creativity which slides behind a constantly changing and generative visible nature. For Ligorio, these 'extravagant paintings' were, in addition, bearers of moral messages – not surprising, perhaps, for he signed himself 'Pirro Ligorio, Hater of the Wicked'.

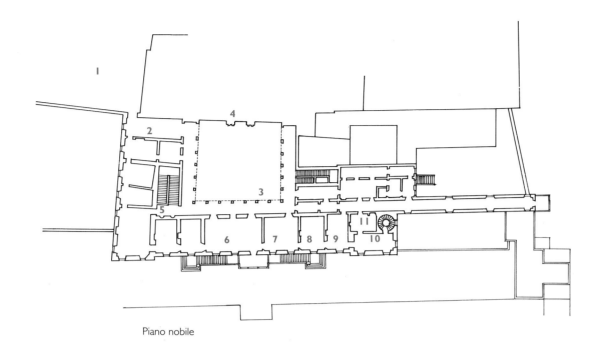

Piano nobile

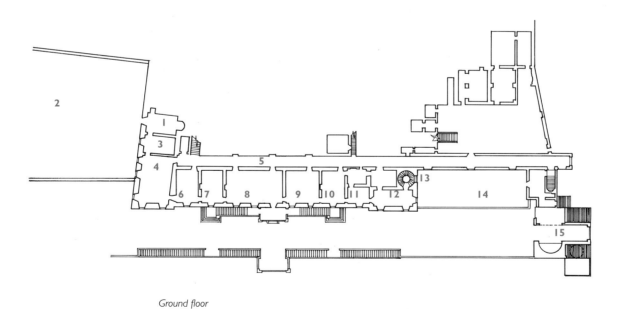

Ground floor

ABOVE: Piano nobile *and ground floor plans, drawing by David Dernie based on a survey by the Soprintendenza per i Beni Ambientali e Architettonici del Lazio.* Piano nobile *(1) Piazza Trento (2) entrance hall (3) courtyard with busts of Emperors (4) Venus Fountain (5) main staircase (6) reception salon (7) antechamber (8) Cardinal's bedroom (9) Cardinal's study (10) gallery (11) chapel;* Ground floor *(1) Cardinal's summer bedroom and Grotto of Venus (2) secret garden (3) Room of Moses (4) Room of Noah (5) corridor (6) Second Tiburtine Room (7) First Tiburtine Room (8) Salotto (9) Room of Hercules (10) Room of Nobility (11) Room of Glory (12) hunting room (13) travertine staircase (14) tennis court (15) dining loggia (with stair to Grotto of Diana below);* OVERLEAF: *View from west showing the old town walls and the supporting structure for the lower gardens*

Mediating between the scale of the garden and the interior of the villa, the Grotesques gave the artist a vehicle with which to demonstrate his capacity to create not only 'like nature', but in the antique manner, thus demonstrating not just his God-given genius of inventiveness, but his virtue of Memory.

Memory, and its embodiment in Mnemosyne, mother of the Muses, is one of the key themes in the garden – not only in the sense that it is understood as the foundation of all the arts, but in a more speculative dimension where the meaning of a particular subject or scene depends on its situation, understood historically. This approach, for which Ligorio is well known, grows out of a humanist philosophical tradition in which understanding is related to *ingenium* (wit, metaphor, imagination). A variability of meaning is brought into play as the *ingenium* of the observer situates the fountain (painting or sculpture) with respect to a broader situation understood in its cultural depth. This means that a particular archaeological fragment can assert a certain identity, but also stand metaphorically for something else at the same time. The topography of the Villa d'Este is not organised rationally, but rather conceived as a complex series of interrelationships – as a journey and as an experience of the place and its history – where the faculty of human *ingenium* discovers both similarity and difference.

The following investigation is not so much a historical discourse as an exploration into the complex and inventive iconography of the garden and villa. As a point of departure it examines contemporary descriptions of the Villa d'Este, attempting in particular to grasp its relation – both thematic and geometric – to the Tiburtine landscape, with its rich reserves of antique ruins.

At the heart of the landscape is the Fountain of the Dragon. Structured like a cave and cut deep into the garden's steep slope, it is the scene of a most powerful drama whose meaning unifies and gathers the most erudite of distant references involved in the pagan imagery. It lies immediately below an important horizon which cuts across the artificial landscape of the garden, creating something of a division – like a fragmented cornice. Conceived to represent the journey between Tivoli and Rome, this horizon symbolises the legendary journey of the Tiburtine Sibyl, a prophetess said to have been found at the foot of Tivoli's famous cascades.

The text will explore the three principal fountains which structure this horizon of the sibyl's journey: the Water Organ, the first of several hydraulic organs to be built in this period; the Oval Fountain, where the sibyl – like Mnemosyne – was framed by mounds of stone to recreate Mount Helicon, and the Rometta, a model of antique Rome and Tivoli. The axial relationships that at first appear to characterise the garden's layout come to be less significant than the primary themes which are in fact played out across this horizon of the sibyl's journey (*see* p65).

Not only is this journey like an armature, uniting an intricate geometry which weaves the fabric of the villa into the ancient landscape, but it is part of an intense struggle to achieve the synthesis of explicit structure and implicit meaning later characteristic of the Baroque. It would be a mistake to consider the garden as lacking 'unity': rather, it is an ingenious attempt to aggregate the antique Tiburtine landscape with classical, local and Estense legend. The unity of intention is first stated powerfully as a visual drama at the Fountain of the Dragon and then completed as a journey in which the inventive imagination discovers successive pieces of a complex game, each unveiling an instructive message at the heart of the garden's artificial landscape, and together synthesising the emblematic references of the Christian journey through life itself.

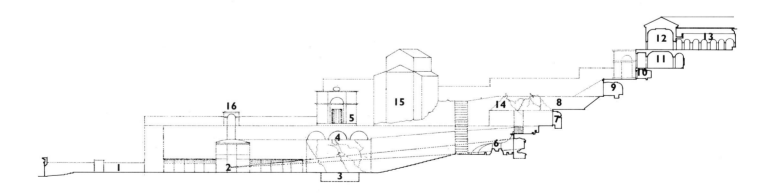

Section, partial reconstruction (sight lines from the entrance to the Fountain of the Dragon shown dotted), drawing by David Dernie based on a survey by the Soprintendenza per i Beni Ambientali e Architettonici del Lazio (1) main entrance, Viale della Prospettiva (2) octagonal pavilion (3) fish pools (4) Grottoes of the Sibyl (5) Water Organ (6) Fountain of the Dragon (7) reclining Hercules (8) Hercules with Telephus (9) Fountain of Pandora (10) Fountain of Leda (11) Salotto – secret garden on this level (12) reception hall – Cardinal's apartments (13) courtyard (14) Oval Fountain (15) Church of S Pietro della Carità (16) Fountain of Venus Cloacina

Diana of Ephesus (originally located at Water Organ)

Axonometric, partial reconstruction, drawing by David Dernie based on a survey by the Soprintendenza per i Beni Ambientali e Architettonici del Lazio

FLUMEN ANIO

Plan showing principal archaeological sites, drawing by David Dernie (1992) based on an archaeological survey by Professor Giuliani Cairoli (1) Temple of the Tiburtine Sibyl (2) Temple of Hercules (3) Grotto of Neptune and Grotto of Sirene at foot of cascade (4) Temple of Hercules Saxanus (5) Villa Quintillius Varus (6) Temple of Hercules Victor – which Ligorio identifies as Villa Augustus (7) Tiburtine amphitheatre (8) Rocca Pia; Villa d'Este (9) Fountain of Venus Cloacina (10) octagonal pavilion (11) Fountain of Neptune (author's interpretation) (12) Fountain of the Dragon (13) Water Organ (14) Grotto of Venus (15) Grotto of Diana (16) Fountain of the Owls (17) Rometta

Ligorio's Tiburtine Antiquities

Efforts to unravel the complex meaning of the Villa d'Este are hindered by the fact that no original description or drawings of the garden exist.[7] As a result Etienne Du Pérac's well-known engraving, published in Rome in 1573, has assumed the authority of a representation of the intended design of the gardens (see p26). Whilst this finely detailed image is invaluable, it is also misleading, at times clearly incorrect, and by no means complete.[8] It was prepared from a drawing Du Pérac made for Emperor Maximilian II and accompanied by a legend which specifically states that its purpose is simply to describe the engraving.

Du Pérac (1525-1604) was an eminent French architect, painter and engraver. He travelled to Rome at the end of the 1550s and stayed for twenty years, becoming well known for his topographical studies. Whether his engraving of the Villa d'Este was based on a missing original is a vexing question: there is little evidence of the existence of such a drawing, and at the same time there are several drawings, for example those in the so-called *Du Pérac Codex*, in which he anticipated projects under construction, and did not necessarily project the scheme as planned, resulting in ideal rather than accurate topographical records.[9] Despite the inventive character of Du Pérac's work, the persuasiveness of his engraving of the Villa d'Este – a sort of flattened-out axonometric which emphasises the axial structure – has prompted the view that the garden's meaning is primarily structured across its two transverse axes. The drama of the landscape and the experience of the garden as a sequence of settings, paths and key horizons give way to a vision almost entirely governed by a matrix of axes.

The garden faces northwest and was built against a steep hill which runs diagonally across the line of the villa. This natural landscape was transformed: a plateau was built along the lower edge and the height of the southeast corner was increased, culminating in a large rocky mound behind the statue of the Tiburtine Sibyl at the Oval Fountain. According to Du Pérac, the lower cross-axis was marked by a line of fish pools stretching between the Water Organ and the Fountain of Neptune (which was never built). Nature's creativity was represented by the two figures of Neptune (ruler of the oceans) and Diana of Ephesus (goddess of nature), or *Mater Matuta*, who surveyed Neptune's domain from the top of a cliff-like facade in the central niche of the Water Organ.

The second prominent cross-axis in Du Pérac's engraving cuts across the hillside at a higher level and is marked by the so-called Line of a Hundred Fountains, which stretches uninterrupted between the Oval Fountain to the east, and the miniature Rome of the Rometta, built out from the ancient town wall to the west. The Oval Fountain is a vision of Tivoli represented as a new Mount Helicon – home of the Muses – looking towards Rome; the great patron of the noble arts. Seen in this way, the upper cross-axis articulates the geographical relationship between Tivoli and Rome and themes associated with poetry and the arts.

A further set of themes emphasised by Du Pérac concerns the legendary figure of Hercules. The French humanist Marc-Antoine Muret, a companion of the Cardinal, wrote several Latin poems in which he dedicated the garden to two Greek heroes, Hippolytus and Hercules, and Du Pérac describes a seated Hercules, the principal deity of Tivoli, as occupying the central niche of the Fountain of the Dragon. Ovid recounts how Hercules, the son of Alcmena and Jupiter, was thrown into fury by Juno, who was out to revenge Jupiter's infidelity, and in that induced state he killed his own children. The oracle Apollo Pizio ordained that Hercules put himself under the servitude of his cousin Eurystheus, for whom he was to undertake his labours, feats of tremendous strength and courage. In return, Apollo promised Hercules immortality. The sequence of Hercules' labours, which often feature in Renaissance fresco cycles, represent the victory of the spirit progressively liberated from the body and from passion until its final apotheosis into heaven. The garden can be interpreted as an allegory of the paradigmatic life of Hercules, where the choice – between the relatively easy path from the Fountain of the Dragon to the Grotto of Venus (Voluptus) and the relatively steep path to the Grotto of Diana (Virtù) high up in the southwest corner of the garden – reflects Hercules' legendary choice between virtue and vice.

In illuminating these themes, the Du Pérac engraving is indeed useful. However, given the scanty evidence upon which the original engraving and its accompanying description were based, it is necessary to compare it with other contemporary descriptions in order to gain a more complete picture. A simple observation of the garden and the surrounding landscape as it appears today is also worthwhile, for, like Du Pérac, later observers of the garden have failed to illustrate that its central axis was in fact built askew to the perpendicular of the villa. Considering the enormous destruction of property and massive earthworks entailed in preparing the artificial contours of the garden, it would surely have been possible to construct a central axis in alignment with the facade of the villa; almost without exception, the Italian villas of the sixteenth and seventeenth centuries were carefully aligned with a geometry which reflected the order and harmony of the heavens.[10] A perspective of the garden, painted in the Salotto in 1567 by Girolamo Muziano (1528-92), provides some indication of the developments which led to such a dramatic shift in garden design.

Unlike Du Pérac, Muziano was probably working under the direct instruction of the Cardinal's erudite humanist court, who would have prescribed the iconographic programme of the frescoe just as Annibal Caro did at the Villa Farnese at Caprarola. Whilst this image correlates with Du Pérac's engraving in some detail, it takes a very different viewpoint, as a distorted perspective seen from an elevated horizon in the east. On the opposite wall is a fountain niche with a mosaic panel representing the ancient Roman Temple of the Sibyl on the Tiburtine Acropolis. Its relationship to Muziano's distorted perspective echoes the actual relationship between the garden and Tiburtine Acropolis and underlines Ligorio's influence on the garden's layout; its meaning was founded on a systematic unfolding of its layered context, the Tiburtine landscape, its topography, antiquities, pagan deities and legends. In Ligorio's words, the endeavour to exhume the antique from its grave was to give it life and invigorate the new:

> Since I realised that many things from antiquity have been left in darkness and buried under the ruins, I thought that it was dignified to remember them, for noble effect, to re-present them to the light and to gather them together.[11]

That this historical, cultural and geographical context underscored the iconographic programme of the garden is implied by Umberto Foglietta, humanist in the Estense court, who in his description of the garden wrote:

> the disposition of the fountains does not only serve to beautify the place and delight the eyes, but also hides in itself a very fine meaning: the portrayal of the nature of the Tiburtine region. This has been thought by my close friend Pyrrhus Ligorius.

Like the structure of the Salotto frescoes, could the skewed axis be concerned with this portrayal of the Tiburtine region?

Of particular relevance to this question is a manuscript by Ligorio which to date has attracted little attention. The 'Descrittione della superba et magnificentissima Villa Tiburtina Hadriana di M Pirro Ligorio' began with a survey of the Tiburtine antiquities surrounding the garden.[12] After giving a history of the founding of Tivoli, Ligorio described the famous temple of the 'Albunia Nympha dell'Acqua Albunea', as well as the temples of Vesta and Hercules above the rocks of the cascade of the Aniene river:

> the river falls into the cave from above, and then into the valley filled with waters, which terrifies the souls of onlookers; for this reason locals have called this place inferno (hell).

Ligorio then described the Temple of Hercules (il principale Dio di questi popoli) on the site of the present cathedral church of Tivoli, the Villa Manlius Vopiscus, the Sabine hills, the Temple of Hercules Victor (which he identifies as the Villa of Augustus), and finally the Tiburtine amphitheatre.[13]

The twentieth-century scholar of architectural history, Marcello Fagiolo, introduced the idea that there was some alignment between the garden and the Tiburtine antiquities.[14] An accurate analysis of this idea proves fruitful, and the various alignments which do exist between the garden and the Tiburtine landscape have such a startling consistency that there seems to be little possibility of their being either casual or coincidental. Quite the contrary; it appears in fact that the placement of the principal fountain elements is determined by a matrix of alignments which thread across the ancient landscape. The Grotto of Diana

is located by a diagonal line struck from the Temple of Hercules Saxanus through the position of the Water Organ (built adjacent to the Church of S Pietro della Carità). This diagonal line bisects the central axis of the garden at the principal niche of the Fountain of the Dragon, and from this point there is a second diagonal joining the new bay in the boundary wall to the central hall of the Villa of Augustus. Extrapolated in the other direction from the niche in the Fountain of the Dragon, the same line locates the entrance on the central axis of the secret garden and the line of the Grotto of Venus in the villa. Furthermore, if a line is extrapolated from the Grotto of Neptune (which lies below the Temple of the Sibyl) perpendicular to the central axis of the garden, the positions of the octagonal pavilion of the lower garden and the centre of the bay in the town walls are located.

Finally, the skewed central axis appears to be generated by its alignment with the town's Roman amphitheatre, and in fact the much-damaged fresco of the Villa d'Este in the loggia of the Palazzina Gambara at the Villa Lante illustrates this relationship. The fresco, which is attributed to the same Zuccaro workshop that carried out many of the frescoes at Tivoli (and therefore to a group conversant with the garden's iconography), has in the background a prominent curved structure which can only be a reconstruction of the Roman amphitheatre adjacent to the Rocca Pia at Tivoli. This is shown directly in line with the garden's central axis. In the garden itself, the skewed line bisects the oval form of the Tiburtine amphitheatre.

For the most part, these relationships can be seen from the balcony of the Salotto or the Cardinal's apartments. In the sixteenth century the landscape would have appeared very different from today. The ancient ruins would have been much more evident amongst the town's buildings: over the freshly planted trees, the Cardinal's guests could have surveyed the garden's alignment with the Villa of Augustus to the northwest, the Villa Quintillius Varus (in line with the skewed central axis), and the Temple of Hercules Saxanus to the northeast, following the Roman road between Rome and Tivoli which ran between the ancient monuments and on to the Tiburtine Acropolis. The Temple of the Sibyl, far to the right of the balcony, would not have been visible because of the rise of the land between the garden and the temple. The Fountain of Pegasus does lie on the invisible line which joins the Cardinal's balcony to the Temple of the Sibyl, and in practical terms, this could have been easily aligned using the high point of the hill which separates the temple from the garden. A simple method for such surveying is set out by Alberti.

Ligorio's misidentification of the Temple of Hercules Victor as the Villa of Augustus was probably the result of an overemphasis on certain inscriptions which referred to Hercules as Augustus – the cult of Hercules was combined with that of the Emperors. It allowed Ligorio to recall the history of the great Roman villas in the Tiburtine region, and

View from balcony of Cardinal's apartments towards the campanile marking the location of the Temple of Hercules Saxanus

more specifically the connection between the Villa of Augustus and the Temple of Hercules Saxanus, both of which can be seen from the Cardinal's balcony. Here, it is said, Hercules stood in the niche in the centre of the nave and gave his orations to the people of Tivoli. And according to Suetonius, Augustus was also noted to hold court in the Temple of Hercules:

> For retirement he went most frequently to places by the sea and the islands of Campagnia, or to the towns near Rome, such as Lanuvium, Praeneste or Tibur, where he very often held court in the colonnades of the Temple of Hercules.[15]

In the sweeping vista between the Villa Augustus and the Temple of Hercules there is an implicit theme of Justice relating to Hercules, Augustus and the Cardinal (as governor of Tivoli), and this is focused on the central niche of the Fountain of the Dragon where, as described below, a white marble statue of Jupiter symbolised the Final Judgement.

It is interesting to see the development of Ligorio's architectural thinking between this attempt to secure the memory of the past in the new gardens at Tivoli and the way he worked to maintain the same relationship at the Vatican Casino for Pius IV.[16] The first and quite obvious correlation between the Villa d'Este and the Casino, and one which has received surprisingly little attention, is the unusual alignment of the Casino. The short axis of the new oval courtyard runs northeast to southwest, bearing little relation to Bramante's Belvedere court, which runs almost north to south. As with the Villa d'Este, the key to its orientation may lie in its alignment with one of the antique ruins indicated in the vicinity in Ligorio's map of Rome (1561), and more explicitly drawn in the area of *Campus Vaticanus* as Villa L Rustii in Du Pérac's map, *Urbis Romae Sciographia* (1574). Here, the ruin is shown with an oval courtyard and two portals on the long axis, in fact strikingly similar to the actual form of Ligorio's Casino. Ligorio was probably working with a structure already begun by Paul IV, and at a practical level it would have seemed sensible to employ the foundations of an earlier building. However, he was no doubt also concerned to 'ground' the *nymphaeum* in the historical context, not only by means of the literary and mythical themes of its stucco work and statuary, but by its orientation with the structures of ancient Rome – just as he had used elaborate geometry to tie the Villa d'Este with the ruins of Tivoli.

The creative thinking which characterised Ligorio's archaeology – and which was the driving force behind the striking departure in garden design in the sixteenth century – depended on the development of the art of perspective and scenography. Of particular interest is the work of Jacopo Barozzi da Vignola (1507-73), whose designs for the Farnese gardens on the Palatine, the formal garden of the Villa Lante at Bagnaia, the Villa Farnese at Caprarola, and the *nymphaeum* of the Villa Giulia all have a deliberately worked relationship to their context. The towns of Caprarola and Bagnaia were restructured to align with the entrances of the new villas; the *nymphaeum* of the Villa Giulia was placed at the end of a river route from the Vatican as one of a number of elements within a wooded valley, and the grotto sequence of the unfinished Farnese gardens on the Palatine involved intricate perspectival orientations, twisted towards the massive ruins of the Basilica of Maxentius across the valley. Vignola brilliantly addressed the problem of siting these villas as a constructed scene which worked between the architecture and its context – not only in historical terms, but with a sense of the local legend of the place – as illustrated by the relationship between the circular courtyard and the nearby Lago di Vico at Caprarola (the legendary creation of which by Hercules is painted on the soffit of the first floor loggia). Vignola was an expert in perspective, first learnt in the Bolognese mathematical circles around Luca Pacioli then mediated through Baldassare Peruzzi (1481-1537), who was in Bologna between 1521-25, a few years after Leonardo had completed his anamorphic drawings in the town. The tradition would have reached Vignola whilst he was working on the gardens of François I de Valois at Fontainebleau between 1540-43. Benvenuto Cellini (1500-71), who was at Fontainebleau at the same time, had brought a copy of Leonardo's important treatise outlining the method of multiple viewpoints; a method fully exploited by Vignola in the Sala del Concilio at Caprarola.[17]

What is important to recognise here is that the perspective allows the garden setting to be grasped in its full depth, as a visual experience whose geometrical consistency embodies a sequence of thematic relationships which build the identity of the garden in its historicity. Whilst working on the garden, Ligorio was also involved in writing his book on rivers and fountains.[18] Drawing on classical, medieval and Renaissance texts, he discussed each river in terms of its philology, the historical events in which it played an important role, and the legends relevant to the pagan deities with which it was associated. Ligorio's textual descriptions are structured like his allegorical sketches, carefully identifying appropriate gestures and figural arrangements to construct the full meaning of the topic. In his *Dance of Salome*, such a grouping is framed architecturally in what appears to be more like a fragment of a garden than an entire room. The space focuses on a distant figure seen in perspective through a deep window, whilst diagonally across to the left, the main space is twisted, opening to spaces outside of the drawing.

In effect, the drawing is completed by the conditions 'drawn in' by the perspective, much like the geometric order of the Villa d'Este, which coordinates the layered themes – erudite, distant, and at times obscure – that contribute to the identity of the garden's fountains, and so finally weaves together the meaning of the complex topography within its historical and geographical context.

The result is an emphasis on a meaning which is *specific* to the context and its history; pertaining not only to the confines of the garden itself, but to the Tiburtine region and to Rome. Like the meaning of the word (*verbum*) in the revived art of rhetoric, the iconography of the late sixteenth-century garden is determined by its 'context' and is therefore variable. The tradition of scenography and perspective – coming through Uccello, Leonardo, Serlio and Vignola – provides the vehicle for considering the whole as a synthetic visual phenomenon, securing the specific meaning of the iconographic programme of the villa with respect to the deep context of the Tiburtine landscape.

The inventiveness in the fields of perspective, poetry, music and archi-tectural settings during the late sixteenth century reflected the increasing independence of the *ingenium* of the artist. And just as the 'context' of the word implied its 'historicity' (hence Dante's use of the Florentine dialect, for instance), so the inventiveness of the artist tended to be stabilised in reference to the historical context. At the Villa d'Este there is a complex attempt to 'ground' the highly artificial landscape of the garden and villa in classical mythology, and more specifically in local Tiburtine history; learning oriented to the *contemplatio* and *admiratio* of history.

FROM LEFT TO RIGHT: Ligorio, panel grotesques; Ligorio, facade perspective

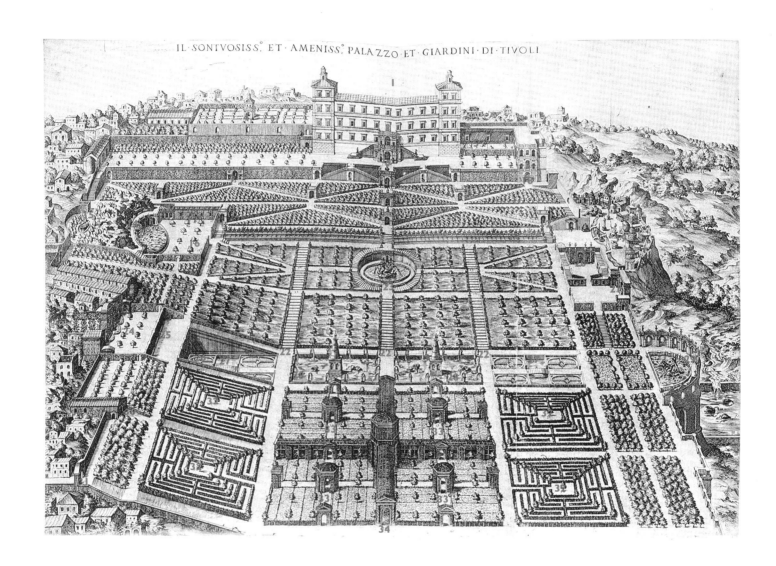

Du Pérac, engraving, 1573 (numeration taken from the Du Pérac legend): (1) villa (2) secret garden (3) Fountain of the Unicorn (4) pavilion (5) tennis court (6) Fountain of Leda (7) Fountain of Thetis (8) Fountain of Aesculapius and Hygieia (9) Fountain of Arethusa (10) Fountain of Pandora (11) Fountain of Pomona (12) Fountain of Flora (13) Line of a Hundred Fountains (14) Oval Fountain (15) Fountain of Pegasus (16) Fountain of Bacchus (17) Grotto of Venus (18) Grotto of Diana (19) Fountain of Rome (20) Fountain of the Emperors (21) Fountain of the Owls (22) Stairs of the Bubbling Fountains (23) Fountain of the Dragon (24) Water Organ (25) Grottoes of the Sibyl (26) Fountain of Antinous (27) fish pools (28) fish pools with Mete Sudanti (29) Fountain of Neptune (30) Fountain of Venus Cloacina (31) Fountain of Triton (32) labyrinths (33) herb gardens (34) entrance below engraving (35) small lakes outside garden

Cardinal's private chapel, sibyl and prophet detail

Temple of the Sibyl, with Grotto of Neptune, lower left

Ligorio, Dance of Salome

Salotto, detail of southeast corner

Salotto, detail of southwest wall fresco of Villa d'Este. Note central holm oak tree (dedicated to Jupiter), nine birds (nine generations of the world according to the sibyl's prophecy) and peacock in the foreground (symbol of eternal life and the resurrection of Christ)

Room of Hercules, soffit fresco showing twelve feats of Hercules and Council of the Gods

Room of Hercules, detail of northeast wall showing Hercules slaying the seven-headed Lernaean hydra

The Fountain of the Dragon: Jupiter's Crystal Cave

At the heart of the garden, as the symbolic focus of the Tiburtine landscape, is the Fountain of the Dragon – so called because of the monstrous four-headed dragon in the centre of its oval pool. It is cut deep into the earth at the foot of the garden's steep slope, to create an oval cave-like space characteristic of the chthonic orientation of the Mannerist period, in which the articulation of a space or painting tended almost to struggle out of a predominantly dark and entrapping field.[19] This, the principal fountain of the garden, gathers and illuminates the meaning of the whole as a visual drama whose layered intentions only unfold at the end of the journey from the lower entrance – where it is framed by the cross-shaped arbour – to the upper terraces of the villa.

The fountain's oval enclosure is framed by a double retaining wall which houses stairs working up either side: these give onto a lateral path halfway up and finally converge over the principal niche which overlooks the lower garden. The staircases were framed by a stream of water flowing between connecting basins carved in the forms of dolphins and shells: contemplation of the soaring central jet was punctuated by intermittent thundering blasts, a hydraulic invention to accompany the gigantic dragon.

The immediate illusion (given the proximity of Hercules) is that the dragon represents the many-headed dragon which the hero slayed as one of his labours to recover the golden apples from the Garden of the Hesperides: '*Ab insomni non custodita dracone*' reads one of the Cardinal's impresa – implying that these apples, often interpreted as virtues, are now in the keep of the Cardinal.[20]

There is another illusion, however, which involves the identity of the fountain's principal niche, dug deep into the hillside towards the Line of a Hundred Fountains. The Du Pérac legend describes the central niche of the fountain as occupied by 'a colossal form of Hercules with his club in hand'. Largely because of this remark, the fountain has without exception been identified with Hercules. Hercules was not only the patron deity of Tivoli, and the mythical ancestor of the d'Este family,[21] but was in a more general sense something of a paradigmatic Renaissance figure who heralded the path to salvation – a symbol of the victory of virtue over vice. With Hercules in this dark niche, it follows that the meaning of the garden can be interpreted as a journey which divides at the Fountain of the Dragon. Here, negotiating the garden's difficult steep slopes, the main path forks between a commodious but shameful journey to the Grotto of Venus, and the path to the Grotto of Diana. The journey through the garden begins at the principal entrance (near the Porta Oscura on the northwest boundary) and ascends towards the Fountain of the Dragon, replaying Hercules' moment of decision, his legendary choice to atone for the terrible sin of slaying his own children.

However plausible this interpretation seems, there is good reason

to inquire further, for there is no mention of Hercules occupying the fountain's central niche in any other contemporary text describing the garden. Like much of the garden, the Fountain of the Dragon was far from complete at the time of Du Pérac's engraving (1572). Zappi, for instance, described its brickwork as not yet stuccoed, and the stairs circumscribing it as unfinished. Together with Audebert, he remarked at length on the thundering noise of the water, whilst Montaigne described a noise which 'issues as of cannon shots'. He continued:

> Were it not for the muddied river water, the fountain would be incomparable … of the finest manufacture and more beautiful to look at with its dependencies than any other thing either in this garden or elsewhere.[22]

All that can be assumed is that the dragons were in place and working for the visit of the newly elected Pope Gregory XIII in 1573.

Given its incomplete state, it is not surprising that Foglietta hardly mentioned the fountain (1569). But it was not even itemised as a fountain in the 1572 inventory, which noted two marble statues of Hercules; one recumbent with a lion's skin and a second, nude, standing beside a stag with Telephus, his son, in his arms. These were both in the second room of the Grotto of Venus, but there is no record of the seated Hercules in either the 1572 inventory or the two inventories published by Seni. Neither Zappi nor Audebert mentioned the presence of statuary at the fountain and, given the detail of the rest of their accounts, it can perhaps be assumed that there was none until after the date of their writing – that is, until after 1576. The lack of any other reference to the seated Hercules would suggest that the Du Pérac legend is in fact mistaken, not even describing an original intention which was simply not executed. Many other less important statues were in the garden at the time, albeit mostly in storage. If this is so, despite the unequivocal opinion in favour of Du Pérac's legend to date,[23] it raises the important question of what was intended for the central niche.

Writing at the beginning of the seventeenth century, the Tiburtine chronicler Antonio Del Re contradicted Du Pérac's description, and in a detailed account offered this interpretation: 'placed high up is a white marble statue of Jupiter sitting on a square seat, partly clothed and partly nude, with leather shoes beautifully laced … and with a lightning bolt in his raised left hand'. The other two niches 'are still unfinished, but there will be things related to Jupiter … something concerning Jupiter is painted in *sgraffito* on each of the walls of these niches'. He continued, describing the niche of Jupiter as containing five secondary niches:

> On the right side, starting from the large niche which holds the statue of Jupiter, there is a painting of the scene when the Titans fought against Jupiter; on the second niche is the scene in the house of Thetis when Minerva and the other gods made a chain to entrap Jupiter, who called Briareus for help and terrified his enemies; on the third niche is painted the scene when Jupiter, in the form

of a swan, seduced Leda; on the fourth niche, the scene when Jupiter was born and Ops, his mother, hid him and trusted him to the Cureti, people of Crete, who made noises with kettledrums and other instruments so that his father Saturn did not hear Ops' wails in the fields, nor the cries of the baby. Had he done so he would have eaten the baby, in accordance with the pact that he had made with his brother Titan . . . On the adjacent wall is painted the Rape of Helen, daughter of Jupiter, by Paris. On the left side of the first wall is depicted the war of the Giants, born of the blood of the stricken Titans, half-snakes, who pitched mountain above mountain to banish Jupiter from the sky. Out of fear Jupiter transformed himself and other gods into animals and escaped, hiding in Egypt. On the second wall Jupiter is represented dividing the world with his brothers, Neptune and Pluto; and then there is the scene when Jupiter transformed himself into golden rain and entered the room in the fortress where the virgin Danae was kept and raped her. On the third wall is Jupiter's kidnapping of the young Trojan Ganymede, whom he loved indecently. On the fourth wall, the death of Jupiter and his burial in the Cretan town, Avlatia. On the fifth and last is a sleeping Venus, another daughter of Jupiter, and a satyr who looks admiringly at her.

Del Re's careful observations are supported by an anonymous document, written between 1609-12 and published by Seni in 1902, which states that the *Piazza delli Draghi* was painted with *The history of Jupiter, foliage and other embellishments*.[24] Together these accounts confirm that at the turn of the seventeenth century a white marble statue of Jupiter was housed in the central niche of the Fountain of the Dragon, and that the enclosure was painted with scenes relating to his life. In this light, the winged dragons have a double meaning. Not only do they refer to the serpent-dragon which guarded the legendary Garden of the Hesperides, but their thunder is a powerful complement to the image of an angered Jupiter.[25]

Perhaps Ligorio had in mind a further inventive allusion tying the oval form of the fountain to that of an amphitheatre open to the sky: the open oval enclosure of the fountain is inscribed with a path or track, and it was originally guarded by four gladiator figures who stood in front of the fountain overlooking the lower garden.[26] In his only published work, *Circi, Theatri, & Anfitheatri*, printed in Venice in 1553 while he was employed at Tivoli, Ligorio said that there was along the spine of the *Circo Massimo* 'the first and principal circus', a temple dedicated to Jupiter: 'The circus was principally dedicated to the sun whose temple was in the middle. On top of the pediment was his shining image . . . And they say that such a place derives its name from Circe, daughter of the sun'.[27] Ligorio stressed the association of the form and open structure of the circus with its dedication to the sun, and it would have been in the character of Ligorio's archaeological inventiveness to imply that the oval,

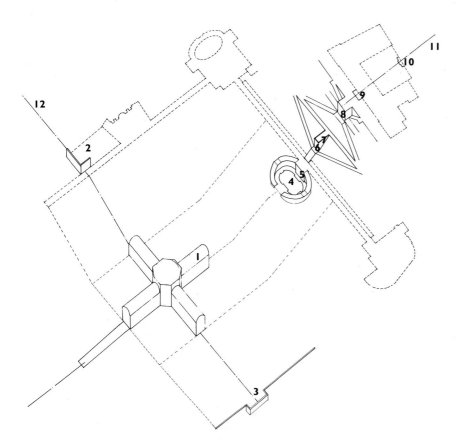

PAGES 34-35: Fountain of the Dragon; ABOVE: Schematic axonometric, drawing by David Dernie (1) cross-pergola (2) Fountain of Venus Cloacina (3) Fountain of Neptune (author's interpretation) (4) Fountain of the Dragon (5) Niche of Jupiter (6) aged Hercules, recumbent (7) Hercules with Telephus (8) Fountain of Pandora (9) Fountain of Leda (10) Fountain of Venus and Constantine (11) alignment to Tiburtine amphitheatre (12) alignment to Temple of the Sibyl. Note: (2) and (3) relate to the salvation of Ino and her transformation into the water deity Leucothea; (5), (6) and (7) also relate to the salvation and apotheosis of Hercules as Christ type

Fountain of the Dragon, detail

Fountain of the Dragon from lower garden

open cave of the Fountain of the Dragon aligned with the Tiburtine amphitheatre and referred to the same themes: a symbol of the sun, and earth, and a temple of Jupiter.

The relationship between the Roman circus and the Fountain of Leda, which is also situated on the central axis, in the niche underneath the stairs to the Salotto, appears in the same text. Ligorio quoted Varro's interpretation of the oval stones on the spine of the circus:

> The eggs which were seen in the circus were dedicated to Castor and Pollux, sons of Jupiter, because according to the poets, they were born from the swan's eggs, that is of Jupiter when he seduced Leda.

Under her left arm Leda held a vase into which a disc of white iron had been inserted, so that when water surged through the gap between the rim and the iron disc:

> ... the water took the form of brilliant rays full of such diverse forms and figures that the sight was dazzling, and in this way, in this place, the sun was imitated and came to represent Jupiter.[28]

To sixteenth-century mythographers, Jupiter represented the divine mind; he was the producer and governor of all things; 'that which they commonly called God'.[29] He had three kingdoms to oversee: the sky (he was most commonly known as *Dio Harmonio*, god of the skies), hell (*Giove Infernale*), and the sea (he is sometimes shown with a trident underneath his feet). On account of this, he was sometimes depicted with three eyes. He shared these kingdoms with his two brothers, Pluto, ruler of the underworld, and Neptune, ruler of the sea. As god of the skies, he orchestrated 'the harmony of the celestial spheres'. He was the principal deity, the 'soul of the world' and nature, because 'from him all things were born and for him lived all that which had life'. Finally, he bore the appellation 'World' since, 'He is all that which is visible and, by his own virtue, he sustains himself . . . In him are all things: earth, water, air, fire, night and day.'[30]

The importance of the omnipotent god Jupiter to the iconography of the garden is echoed in Muziano's Salotto fresco. A holm oak bisects the fresco, cutting the central axis at the start of the steep slope up to the villa. The oak, like the olive tree, was sacred to Jupiter and so was planted all around the Fountain of the Dragon. In the same way as the tree in the fresco structures a division between the lower and upper parts of the garden (and from the date of the fresco, 1565, it is clear that this scheme was planned at an early stage), the Fountain of the Dragon itself mediates between the two levels across the key horizon of the garden marked by the Line of a Hundred Fountains.

The dividing line, which plays a primary role in structuring the garden's overall topography, is first of all represented in the Fountain of the Dragon as a metamorphosis of light and water from the shadowy walls and deep pool of the enclosure to a spectacle of crystal light at the summit of the tall jet. Like the Fountain of the Lanterns at the Villa Lante, the Fountain of the Dragon is cut deep into the steep slope of the garden, with Jupiter set on a travertine throne in a cave with walls of water, tartaro and roughly hewn travertine. Cast in permanent shadow by the tall retaining walls and evergreen holm oaks surrounding the fountain, the white marble statue would have glistened in the darkness of the fountain enclosure, a setting typical of the Mannerist imagination, which was fascinated by the mysterious darkness of the earth. From the dark, cavernous ground, the crystal waters of the fountain's tall jet soared high above the Line of a Hundred Fountains as though they were joining heaven and earth, light and dark – a gesture towards the domain of the Cardinal, whose rooms on the level of the courtyard were painted with personifications of the Virtues, and whose virtuous life reflected divine light on earth.

This representation of the transformation of the garden across the horizon recalls ancient themes in which light was understood as a vehicle of mediation, articulating the infinite distance between earth and heaven. From Neo-Platonism came the sixteenth-century association of light with the continuity of an invisible *anima* or *spiritus mundanus*: 'Light is a property without body (material)', in the words of Lomazzo. Light was reflected by the angels and planets to the earth and there it was infused into the material bodies.[31] Materials themselves represented an entrapment for the soul – to be released in death but revealed on earth in rare and marvellous materials or in materials in a state of transformation: metamorphic rocks, corals and fossils. Just as the zodiacal ceilings of the Chigi Chapel, the Farnesina in Rome or the Farnese Palace at Caprarola coordinated with surety the passage of the planets (God's instruments in the skies), the complementary orientation towards the chthonic attempted to reveal God's presence in the earth: the artist-genius of the sixteenth century shifted the focus of the traditional mediative structure between heaven and earth.

Light (following Ficino) was understood as a manifestation of God's metaphysical substance: '*ubique divinae veritas bonitatisque imago*'. But this '*virtù celeste*' (the term used frequently by Ligorio and others) was reflected by the planets and absorbed by materials which corrupted its pure form. In the shadows of a dark canvas or the walls of an underground room, the Mannerist artist sought to lay bare the veil of material form to reveal the hidden soul of the world, the divine spirit or *anima nascoste* within the earth. This idea was first made explicit at the Fountain of the Dragon in the figure of Jupiter – the embodiment of the generative impulse of all creativity located in the darkest room of the entire garden: a luminous image of the divine spirit in the depths of the earth. Implicitly, the same theme lay behind the fountain's tall jet, as a release of Jupiter's splendour from its imprisonment on earth, a surging jet of glistening water.

Jupiter's dark niche was infused with the warm rays of the sun as they penetrate the humid earth, creating an image typical of sixteenth-century attempts to reify the invisible process of natural creativity. Most frequently, this mysterious process – a witness to God's presence on earth – is associated with the sun, whose warmth is the cause of a generative earth and a transformation of nature 'because the sun works in the earth as a material capable of producing every kind of animal, metal, precious stones and such things'. This description by Boccaccio of the *wisdom* of the earth was emphasised by Bernardo Telesio who, in his *Opuscoli*, stressed the importance of the sun, recognising only the action of its light and warmth on the cold, dark earth as the source of all that exists in nature.

An extraordinary engraving in the influential mythologist Vincenzo Cartari's *Le Imagini De i Dei De Gli Antichi* provides an insight into the imaginative visualisation of *nature creating* as it was understood in the sixteenth century (see p45). The engraving, showing a crocodile in the sea with the 'Ship of the Sun' on its back, was described as representing 'the Principle which governs the Universe: God as the force of the sun fused with humidity in the generation of things, removing the sadness of the latter'.[32] As a reptile, the crocodile represents both earth and water. The warmth of the sun (as Apollo) purges the humid earth of its sadness, generating movement of its nutritive waters. Like blood through the veins of a body, the sun's rays bring the earth to life. In a divinely ordained cycle, the light of the sun (*anima celeste*) is absorbed by the earth and becomes the hidden generative principle, the *anima nascoste*. The soul of the earth is revealed in the open water channels which thread their way down the slopes of the Villa d'Este and in the famous *catena* of the Villa Lante at Bagnaia. In Ligorio's words, 'consider spring water as nutritious and the soul of the substance of all plants'.[33] This notion, which also appears in Bernardo Telesio's *De Rerum Natura*, is explicitly represented in the arrangement of fountains below the platform of the famous dining table in the formal gardens of the Villa Lante. Built into a retaining wall below the outdoor dining room is the Grotto of Neptune (on the left) and the Grotto of Venus (on the right). Between the two is the Fountain of the Lanterns, the circular form of which cuts into the depth of the retaining wall, much like the Fountain of the Dragon at Tivoli. This wall – always in shadow – is like a vision of the dark, generative earth: 'You know that all things generate themselves through warmth and humidity,' wrote Bartoli. 'I have taken Venus to be warmth and Neptune, humidity, so that through these two qualities all the herbs and plants of this garden . . . will multiply and grow'.[34]

The Fountain of the Lanterns is like an image of the sun itself embedded in the earth; flanked by the grottoes representing humidity and warmth, it is embellished with numerous round basins and jets representing the generative soul of the earth. They sparkle in the afternoon sun and announce the giant stone dining table on the level above, where the fruits of the earth were laid out before God.

At the Villa d'Este, a more complex set of relationships structures the garden between the Salotto (which itself was designed like a garden room, with Zuccaro's ceiling perspective opening up a 'Feast of the Gods' scene), and the fountains of Venus and Neptune, which address each other across the lower garden. Framed by an arched espalier, these two fountains (in fact, never built) are brought together as a single visual experience in the octagonal pavilion at the heart of the lower garden: the Grotto of Venus Cloacina to the east, the Fountain of Neptune to the west, and directly ahead, like the Fountain of Lanterns, is the Fountain of the Dragon, cut deep into the earth and creating the garden's tall light-filled water jet. Jupiter's oval cave can be understood as an almost sacred domain embodying an image of divinely inspired natural creativity. The sixteenth-century chthonic made tangible the invisible spirit linking heaven and earth: the shadowy world of the Mannerist imagination was an anxious search for light, and the depths of Jupiter's cavern were veiled in a gently seeping film of water, transparent like crystal.

Like most sixteenth-century grottoes, Jupiter's niche and the walls of the fountain's enclosure were lined with a stone known as tartaro or *spogna*, interlaced with tubes to produce an illusion which recalls the beautiful metaphor of the *Weeping Earth* of Lucretius. Tartaro is a calcium deposit which occurs naturally in the caves alongside the mineral-rich waters of the Aniene; Alberti referred to it as 'travertine foam'. In Esiod's *Teogonia Tartaro*, it was the foundation of the universe, the deepest part of the earth, lying below hell itself, the place of imprisonment of the gods' enemies. The distance between hell and tartaro was equal to the distance between sky and earth. It was one of the world's primordial elements, along with Eros, Chaos and Gaia (earth). Its unification with the earth produced monsters – Tartarus, brother of Sleep (son of the Night), and the winged personification of death. Gradually the material tartaro became equated with hell itself. On the Day of Atonement, according to Saint Augustine's 'City of God', when the blazing sun had extinguished and the radiance of the moon had died, the earth would open up to the sound of a mournful trumpet, revealing a vast abyss of tartaro.

Here, the association of tartaro with an apocalyptic vision coincides thematically with the image of Jupiter, lightning bolt raised aloft, about to judge the fallen world. At the heart of the garden and the Tiburtine landscape is the cave of tartaro, which embodied the joint themes of destruction at the end of time and the regeneration of the purified world. The metamorphosis of this cycle was first envisaged brilliantly by Raphael in a fresco in the Chigi Chapel in S Maria del Popolo in Rome, in which the cloud-like figurations representing the souls of the Chigi brothers appear to float towards the immaterial world of light, held in the depth of the glass mosaic dome.

In the domain of the garden, the theme is embodied in the first room of the Grotto Grande at Boboli (designed by Bernardo Buontalenti in 1585-88), which represents Ovid's tale of Pyrrha and Deucalion, the

Fountain of the Dragon towards the east

Fountain of the Dragon, detail of Niche of Jupiter

only survivors of the Great Flood. After consulting the oracle Themis, they threw stones, 'the bones of our great mother', behind them. The stones began to lose their stiffness and gradually assume shape. Those which contained a little water turned to flesh, and out of the earth, humanity was reborn:

> for when moisture and heat unite, life is conceived, and from those two sources all things will spring. When, therefore, the earth, covered with the mud from the recent flood, became heated by the hot and genial rays of the sun, she brought forth innumerable forms of life, in part, the ancient shapes, and in part, creatures new and strange.[35]

A fascination with the 'chance image' gained impetus in the late sixteenth century, and the 'marvellous' character of the tartaro-clad cave wall itself became a subject for reverie. Tartaro tended to be selected for its specific physiognomy, its potential figurative character: 'bodies brought forth by nature', to quote Alberti. This chance image is a theme mentioned as early as Pliny, who described an agate belonging to Pyrrhus on which Apollo with his lyre and the nine Muses could be seen. It was kept alive in medieval thought, which tended to regard these 'cloud figures' as real; Albertus Magnus claimed that exhalations from the earth, if aided by heavenly constellations, might be able to form the perfect, though lifeless, bodies in the clouds. Leonardo da Vinci's landscapes and battles on stained walls are well known, and several cloud figures can be detected in the work of Mantegna, an expert on gems and stones. Finally, Vasari, writing in the mid-sixteenth century, claimed that the shift from seeing images in materials, real or painted, to actually using the implied image as part of a constructed painting was made by Sebastiano del Piombo, who painted on a variety of materials, rendering their figurations as clouds, or the setting sun.[36]

In the late-sixteenth century, it was thought that the fossil, or petrified life, captured a phase in the natural creative process, and that it was the role of the artist to bring this to light.[37] Similarly, the inventive imagination could bring to life the latent figures in the shapeless surface of a tartaro wall; here, for example, is Laferi's description of the tartaro caves below the Tiburtine cascades:

> with the passage of time, and by its nature, the Aniene river has generated *tartari* of diverse forms, such that in many places they appear joined together, like human figures, at times animals, fruit and infinite marvellous things.

Tartaro – as part water, part stone – embodied the reciprocal power of the earth, which both devours and gives life. The stone lined the walls of the dark arena of the Fountain of the Dragon where Jupiter threatened the fallen world below and, like a baptism, opened the way to a new world purified of sin.[38]

This moment of Judgement – recounted in Ovid's *Metamorphoses* and echoed in Hercules, Augustus, and finally Tivoli's new governor Ippolito – has its obvious parallel in the Book of Genesis, and there are two scenes relating to the Old Testament Judgement in the villa itself; the first, in the frescoed ceiling of the Room of Noah, which depicts Noah's sacrifice after the cessation of the rains, and the second in a biblical scene painted on the soffit of the entrance hall to the courtyard. To symbolise his divine covenant with the earth, God appears to Noah in the form of a rainbow – dramatically recreated in the lower gardens over the pools. The image of Jupiter's tartaro cave then instills a sense of horror, as a scene recalling not only the Ovidian myth but also the story of Noah: the devastation of a world full of sin and the hope for survival.

FROM LEFT TO RIGHT: Cartari, Jupiter dressed in white with a resplendent crown and mantle 'which appears like glass' and is painted with stars. In his right hand he carries two balls, one of gold and the other silver, and his throne is covered with a cloth made of peacock feathers. Under his feet is a trident. He represents Providence, Justice and Divine Goodness; Cartari, The Ship of the Sun

Stair of the Bubbling Fountains

Stair of the Bubbling Fountains, with detail at foot of stairs

The Fountain of Neptune and the Lower Garden

The Fountain of the Dragon overlooked a relatively flat section of the garden which was characterised by a lattice of orthogonal paths and aligned with the principal entrance to the garden on its northern edge, near the Porta Oscura where the Via Tiburtina entered Tivoli. The arrangement of this part of the garden – below a seated, immutable Jupiter surveying a pattern of labyrinths and pools – recalls the northern section of Buontalenti's contemporaneous garden for the Medicis at Pratolino. An engraving of this garden by Venturini (1691) shows a Jupiter with a raised thunderbolt seated at the head of two circular labyrinths, and miniature mountains of tartaro stone (see p50). As at the Villa d'Este, Jupiter is located above the level of the labyrinths, at the highest point of the natural slope of the garden. The circular labyrinths are an ancient symbol describing the four quarters of the earth, and a journey leading towards the domain of the gods. Here, thunderbolt aloft, Jupiter waits to pass judgement on the soul.

Like the path to the summer garden at the Villa Farnese at Caprarola, the approach to the villa through the garden began through a long arched arbour whose wooden structure was covered with vines. From the entrance gate, this shaded passage was flanked by two walls (marked with two rustic fountains) known as the *Viale della Prospettiva*. It continued to form a cross-shaped arbour which divided a herb garden into four. To the west were built two labyrinths (Du Pérac shows two more in the east), while at the centre of the arrangement was a wooden octagonal pavilion. Furnished with stone benches and refreshing fountain jets, this pavilion would have provided visitors to the garden with a place to rest and to contemplate a journey which, in one sense, was a journey from darkness to the light reflected on the upper slopes of the garden. In the afternoon sun, the glistening white marble statue of Jupiter would have been just visible from the pavilion beyond the tall jet of the Fountain of the Dragon (see p16). By way of initiation, the Cardinal's coat of arms were fixed to the underside of the domed roof, and an angered Jupiter bore down onto the visitor about to enter the privileged domain of the Estense villa.

This covered walk ended at the edge of the labyrinths, towards the Fountain of the Dragon. Ahead was a line of unusually deep fish pools (conveniently located in the region of the garden requiring most ground fill to create the level platform above the existing vineyards). Three of the pools were complete by 1576, according to Zappi (although Del Re notes only two): the fourth, illustrated by Du Pérac, was never built and perhaps was never intended. In its place is a pool built as part of the alterations to the Water Organ and a niche housing a partially sculpted figure of Neptune. Zappi described the pools as '*peschiere*', populated with exotic birds and fish, and similarly Audebert called them '*viviers*'. The pools referred to the domain of Neptune, the image of the ocean,

'Father of all the gods. The Universal power of water . . . which was the principle of all things'.[39]

To the west of the pools there was to be a fountain of Neptune, but since it was never built, it is not described in any contemporary account other than Du Pérac's. This shows Neptune in his chariot drawn by sea horses (*hippocampi*) in a semicircular basin, which is cantilevered beyond the old town walls, rivalling the Rometta in scale. Du Perac's location of the fountain at the westernmost end of the fish pools has generally been accepted as accurate.[40] However, the unfinished statue of Neptune (possibly the figure which is today at the foot of the Water Organ) is quite unlike Du Pérac's Neptune. It is likely that Du Pérac conjured a popular image of Neptune and further imagined that it was to be supported by a substantial curved retaining wall.

The present wall shows no evidence that such a curved structure was ever there (see pp14-15). This alone would tend to suggest that, contrary to Du Pérac's engraving, a fountain of this type was never planned for this position. Would it not have been normal practice first to build the supporting structure on the boundary wall? Above all, it would seem unusual to begin carving a colossal figure of Neptune before forming the primary structure for a fountain. Perhaps, as Del Re suggested, the Neptune was destined for a nearby location on the boundary wall. If this is in fact the case, the implications for the iconographic reading of the garden are interesting. The cross-axial arrangement between the Water Organ and the Fountain of Neptune would no longer exist, cancelling the relevance of the ideas which have governed previous interpretations of the garden's iconography.

A location of Neptune somewhere along the boundary walls of Tivoli would coincide with the ancient association of this god with city walls and foundations (Juno is likewise connected with city gates, and Minerva with the rocks and fortress of a city).[41] However, with no precise documentation available, an examination of the layout of the underground water pipes for the garden is the best source of evidence regarding the location of the fountain. A major water supply would have been necessary, but as far as can be deduced, there is no water channel to the position indicated by Du Pérac (a brick channel carries water from the Fountain of the Owls down the slope of the garden and changes direction away from the supposed location). There is no inspection chamber (which might have indicated a provision for a sharp change of direction) and no known channel in the vicinity. In light of the fact that the figure of Neptune was virtually complete – although nothing had been done on the fountain's preliminary works, supporting structure or water supply – it must be concluded that the fountain was never intended to be in the position indicated by Du Pérac. Instead, could it have been intended for the large bay slightly further along the boundary wall, in line with the octagonal pavilion? Here, a substantial structure was built to support the cantilevered bay, shown by both Muziano and by Du Pérac, which is in fact fifteen metres long and four metres deep. Furthermore, there was provision for a large water supply to the bay – its centre coincides with a water chamber which terminates the major water channel of the garden before discharging it into an open channel on the Via Tiburtina.[42] Significantly, a line passing through the centre of the bay, the octagonal pavilion and along the orientation of the cross-axis of the garden cuts through the Grotto of Neptune which, together with the Grotto of the Sirens, is set deep into the travertine cliffs below the ancient Tiburtine Acropolis.

The whole of the Tiburtine landscape below the acropolis was restructured in the nineteenth century, but previously two cascades poured into the valley; the Aniene itself and 'la stipa', a canal which helped to regulate the flow of the Aniene. Tivoli was famous for its waterfalls, which crashed onto the rocks with such a fearsome thunder that the area became known as the *Valle dell'Inferno*.[43] Water from the Aniene, as it fell into a small lake in the valley below the acropolis, would rush into the Grotto of Neptune, deep in the travertine rock below the circular Temple of the Sibyl. On the other side of the lake stood the Villa Manlius Vopiscus.[44] The lake must have recalled the *specchio di Diana* in Nepi, where the cult of Jupiter began much earlier than in Rome. Further to the east, the water ran out through the Grotto of the Sirens, a long and precipitous natural gallery set underneath a naturally carved bridge, Ponte Lupe.

A poem written in 1702 by Lorenzo Lucesse to introduce his description of the Villa d'Este suggests that these natural caves were already associated with Neptune at that time. The poem describes a kind of dialogue between the Aniene and Neptune in which the river tells the god of the marvels of the garden as it flows from Tivoli.[45] Today, the partially restructured grotto is still impressive in its scale, and the drama of the precipitous landscape offers an insight into how it must have appeared in the sixteenth century. This landscape, which Ligorio would have surveyed meticulously, is represented in the garden of the Villa d'Este both literally, on the southern edge of the Rometta, and thematically, in the Water Organ (alternatively described as the Fountain of the Flood). Originally, when the music of the Water Organ came to an end, a torrent of water was released as the aeolic chamber was emptied. The effect was described by Audebert:

> When the music comes to an end, a small rope is pulled which
> unblocks a few pipes, and then a huge quantity of water (enclosed
> in and around the cave) starts to flow all around. There really
> seems to be a tempest or a storm because of the noise caused
> by the strength of the water coming up from underground.

Furthermore, like the Temple of the Sibyl, the vertical organisation of the Water Organ – from the grottoes dedicated to the sibyl to the circular enclosure in front of the organ pipes – supplanted the natural wonder of the Tiburtine landscape with the artificial spectacle

of the Universal Flood. Such fantastical structures were typical of gardens of the period – other examples are the incredible artificial mountain in the Villa Medici in Rome, and Giambologna's giant Appennino at Pratolino. At the Villa d'Este, the natural landscape was taken as an emblem for the apocalyptic flood described in Ovid's *Metamorphoses*:

> Jupiter, not wanting the world and heavens to be consumed by
> fire, as foretold by the Fates, decided to send rains upon the
> earth, and in their deluge drown a sinful human race. He crushed
> the heavy clouds brought forth by the south wind which were
> refilled by Iris, Juno's rainbow-clad envoy 'and storms of blinding
> rain poured down from heaven'.

This rain itself was ingeniously recreated at the level of the pools, which were surrounded by sixteen columns (or fourteen according to Del Re) connected by a travertine cornice. The cornice was pierced by small tubes which threw fine jets of water into the pools, creating the effect of 'a gentle artificial rain', similar to the Fountain of the Deluge at the Villa Lante in Bagnaia, which is still in working order. Audebert described the rainbow created by this arrangement:

> the water flows in abundance, thrusting upwards, joining the
> water from the opposite pillar and creating a semicircle [of wa-
> ter] which gets wider and wider. The sun glistens through it and
> creates a rainbow; in other words, Iris.

This was one of the few fountains which Montaigne complimented unreservedly, describing a 'thick and continuous rain' falling on the pools to create a rainbow 'so natural and distinct that it in no way falls short of what we see in the sky'.[46] And to complete the scene, to the west was the statue of Neptune himself who, according to legend, 'struck the earth, which quaked and moved to give the waters way', sweeping aside man and beast. Ligorio's *Valle d'Inferno* is, like the lower garden of the Villa d'Este, the domain of Neptune, who symbolises the cycle of death and regeneration of life.

An implicit geometry, with Jupiter at its pinnacle, aligns the key elements of the lower garden with the Villa Augustus, the Temple of Hercules Saxanus and the Villa Quintillius Varus. The way of orchestrating the lower garden was a direct reflection of Ligorio's archaeological and artistic inventiveness in combining references from classical and local mythologies with specifically Tiburtine legends. The same inventive character pervades the whole villa.

The focus on Hercules and Jupiter (two statues of Hercules overlook the Fountain of the Dragon) reflects the important cult of their combined worship in ancient Tivoli. This theme is also represented inside the villa, in the so-called First Tiburtine Room (facing the garden), which contains frescoes describing the legends of the founding of Tivoli by the Greek brothers Catillus, Coras and Tiburtus. On the rear wall are scenes linking Hercules with his father, Jupiter: Hercules fights Albio and Bergio to recover stolen cattle. As he tires in battle,

Jupiter showers stones upon his foes. The connection is underlined by the placement of two painted figures, Jupiter and Juno, on either side of the central panel, together with a ceiling painting directly above, which depicts an augury scene: the three founding brothers, guided by Jupiter's thunderbolt, stand beside a holm oak tree dedicated to Jupiter (see pp51-52). Jupiter is not only the saviour of Hercules, but the inspiration for the founding of Tivoli. In the garden these themes are coordinated geometrically with the gods of the sea (Neptune) and the generative earth (Diana of Ephesus). The lower garden's fish pools and fruit trees are flanked by the dramatic representation of the mythical flood on one side, and by Neptune, the figure representing the source and

ultimate end of all things, on the other. The arrangement articulates a parallel between the regeneration of the earth after the flood (the fruit trees, fish pools and exotic birds) and the legendary creation of Tivoli itself. The ancient themes associated with the garden — which Ligorio called 'a paradise on earth' — are keyed to the specific historical and legendary context of the Tiburtine landscape. Against this background, the legends of the Tiburtine Sibyl come to the fore and, after the location of Jupiter's niche and the plotting of the principal orientations with respect to the antique landscape, it was the attempt to represent sibylline legend which determined the garden's layout.

ABOVE, FROM LEFT TO RIGHT: Pratolino Gardens, Jupiter; Cartari, La Gran Madre. The personification of earth is crowned with a tower, her dress is green and patterned with leafy branches, her sceptre is representative of earth ruling over the entire richness of human life and her key represents the opening and closing of the earth according to the seasons. Her carriage is pulled by lions — even the king of all animals is subject to the laws of nature; Tivoli, Grotto of Neptune

First Tiburtine Room, the legendary founders of Tivoli, Catillus, Coras and Tiburtus, landing at Latium (above); scene of the building of Tivoli with the Temple of the Sibyl (below)

First Tiburtine Room; soffit showing Catillus, Coras and Tiburtus making a sacrifice under a holm oak (above); Hercules Saxanus aided in battle by Jupiter's shower of stones, flanked by Jupiter and Juno (below)

Second Tiburtine Room, three river gods, Tiber, Anio and Erculaneo, flanked by personifications of music

The Tiburtine Sibyl

The apocalyptic image of the Universal Flood, which not only embraces the Cave of Jupiter but also forms the focus of the lower garden, involves a temporal iconography, and a passage from one world into the next. The boundary representing this metamorphosis is the curious L-shaped 'middle horizon' of the garden, which starts with the unbuilt Fountain of Venus Cloacina, continues as a level path to the Oval Fountain and then arrives at the Rometta via the Line of a Hundred Fountains. On the one hand, the passage by these fountains is a journey which opens the way to the upper garden – the virtuous domain of the Cardinal; on the other, a story of the Tiburtine Sibyl, the ancient prophetess whose apocalyptic verses foretold the Final Judgement. (see p65).

There are references to the sibyl in each of the principal fountains which structure the middle horizon, but her main statue is housed at the Oval Fountain. In their descriptions of this fountain, Foglietta, Zappi, Lafreri and Del Re recalled the legend of the Albunean Sibyl, involving the myth of Ino and Leucothea from Ovid's *Fasti* (vi 461–82) and *Metamorphoses* (iv 510–42). Ino was the sister of Semele, who was the mother of Bacchus by Jupiter. A jealous Juno induced Semele to request to see Jupiter in all his light. When he appeared before her, Semele was struck down by lightning, but Jupiter saved the child in her womb and sewed him into his own breast, and it was from there that Bacchus was born. The baby was given to Ino, who fostered him. Jealous once more, Juno cast a spell on Ino's husband, Athamas, who went into a rage and, snatching their first son from his wife's arms, wildly smashed the child's head against a granite block (see p58). Ino fled her husband's fury with their second son, Melicertes, and leapt into the Ionian sea. They were saved by Neptune, who transformed them into water deities, Ino becoming Leucothea, and Melicertes, Palaemon, the protector of ports. Leucothea eventually came to the shores of the Tiber near the Foro Boario, where she encountered a group of Bacchante celebrating their rituals in a sacred wood. She was threatened again with violence, and again at the instigation of Juno, she was saved by Hercules. She finally confided in the prophetess Carmenta, who declared that her fate be celebrated as *Mater Matuta*: 'When she now, with the breath of divine spirit upon her, answered to petitioners from the oracle, she was called "Sibylla Tiburs".'

Ligorio described the Albunean Sibyl on two occasions, under the headings Amalthea and Albunea in his *Antiquità*. According to him, Albunea is the name of a fountain, mountain and wood deified by the Italians *as Mater Matuta* or Albunea Sibylla, and known to the Greeks as Leucothea. Ligorio described her as a prophetess whose circular temple was built at Tivoli. Like Saint Augustine, he likened her to the Cumean Sibyl and told of how Tarquinius commanded his troops according to her verses. Foglietta described Albunea as the name given to one of three wells in the Tiburtine region that were the sources of three rivers: the Anio, Erculaneo and Albunea (so called because of its whitish waters). Recounting the writings of Brother Felipo da Bergamo, Zappi described the Tiburtine Sibyl located in the mouth of the Aniene, in the *Valle d'Inferno*; below the circular temple 'was found a statue of natural marble of her likeness, holding a book in her hand'.[47] Legend tells that she was then carried triumphantly to the Roman Campidoglio and to the Temple of Jupiter where the books of the sibyls were kept. There, in the midst of an olive grove, according to an ancient Greek text, the gathered priests told her of their vision of nine suns shining down upon the earth; 'the nine suns are the nine generations,' responded the sibyl. The wise men continued to recount their vision:

> The first sun was multi-coloured, with shining rays . . . enormous, very splendid. The second sun was also shining, multi-coloured, and splendid. The third sun was like blood, like tartaro, very large; a scorching fire. The fourth sun was also like blood, and very luminous; lightning as during a storm with thunder. The sixth was like a cloud, snow and blood. The seventh was like tartaro, and blood. The eighth sun was shining; it seemed to have hands at its centre. The ninth was more like tartaro than the others and it gave out light. [48]

The sibyl explained that the nine suns represented an apocalyptic vision of nine generations of the world, ending with the day of the Final Judgement. The first sun, the first generation, signified a world without sin; the second 'also with honest, mild and hospitable men, without malice', but the third generation was an age of war, when nation would rise against nation, with the exception of the citizens of Rome who would be charitable. The fourth generation of the world was the age of Christ: 'from the land of the Jews will appear a woman called Mary who will give birth to a child who they will call Jesus'.

The sibyl then foretold of the coming of Alexander Seleuco and Herod, the reign of Augustus, and Christ's crucifixion. The fifth sun was to bring three kings, Antiochus, Tiberius and Gaius, who would organise persecutions and rebuild the sanctuaries at Eliopoli and Lebanon. The sixth heralded the reign of Constantine, among others; the seventh, the reign of Arcadius and Onorius, followed by Theodosius and Valentinianus; the eighth, the arrival of 'a king with the name of a beast', which would end in the sack of Rome. Finally, the ninth generation of the world:

> the coming of the Antichrist, the return of Enoch and Elijah on the earth, the elimination of the Antichrist and the final triumph of Christ . . . Then Christ will reign, the son of the living God with his angels.

It is likely that Ligorio had knowledge of the Greek text, for under the voice of Amalthea he related how the Albunean Sibyl spoke of the end of the Republic and of the coming of Christ:

Others say that the Albunean Sibyl was the Cumean Sibyl, who foresaw King Priscus Tarquin's work of greatness and its downfall, and the change of the Republic and its religion. They secretly took many sayings from her and ordered the priesthood in accordance with the sibylline verses, for they found in them that when Rome built bridges of stone and marble on the Tiber, the Republic would fall, and after the building of the Ponte Senetorio [today called Santa Maria] at the end of the Macedonian War, social war would be followed by civil war until the great Augustus became Emperor, and under his reign would be born our Saviour of the Holy Virgin, Emperor of the Skies.[49]

Furthermore, the interior of the villa contains a number of explicit references to the sibyl's prophecies. These appear primarily in the Second Tiburtine Room in frescoes by Girolamo Muziano and Cesare Nebbia relating to the mythical founding of the ancient city of Tibur (see pp57-61). In the centre of the vaulted room is Apollo, the sun god, in a chariot drawn by four white horses and genii holding flaming torches. Four smaller panels radiating from the central image depict Muses identified with music and poetry. Related to these, below the cornice, are small figures representing the cardinal virtues, and woven in between these images, in a sequence resembling something of a labyrinth, are panels at the lower and upper level recounting the myth of Ino. She is first seen fleeing with Melicertes from the fury of Athamas in an oval image over the window to the garden. Her first son, about to be slain, glances over to Venus on the opposite wall. Venus calls upon her father, Neptune, to save the drowning Ino and child. Transformed into Leucothea and Palaemon, they are depicted to the right of the image of the Venus, whose carriage, in the form of a shell, is drawn across the sea by a dolphin. Above this group is King Anio, drowning in a desperate attempt to save his daughter from being led away by Mercury.[50]

Finally, the two lateral walls of this room show the sibyl on her journey from the Tiburtine cascades to Rome – a depiction ingeniously recreated as a journey around the middle horizon of the garden, where the nine generations of time are laid out as nine paths which regulate the lower garden in both directions (see p65).

As a prophetess, the sibyl takes her place among the Old Testament prophets in the Cardinal's Chapel, but she is also implicitly invoked in several frescoes around the villa which contain references to the number nine, in the form of figures, birds or animals. In the Second Tiburtine Room the sibyl is accompanied by nine goats, and there is a total of nine figures in the scene representing Venus and Neptune. The dragons of the impresas over each of the four doors have respectively eight, nine, ten and eleven heads; the same numerical reference appears in a small detail in Muziano's perspective of the garden in the Salotto. This image is divided by a holm oak, the tree sacred to Jupiter, which in turn divides the flight of nine birds – eight to the right of the tree, and the ninth (a bird of paradise representing the world cleansed of sin) flying towards the upper garden and domain of the Cardinal. The same nine birds appear in the stucco panel which (according to Del Re) represented Pan and Syrinx in the Grotto of Diana.

The caprice of the birds alludes not only to the numerical symbolism of the sibyl's prophecies, but to her legendary association with Apollo, who is painted in the main ceiling panel in the Second Tiburtine Room. The sibyls were said to have knowledge of the oracles of Apollo, and it is recounted that the Tiburtine Sibyl (often with the Cumean and Eritrean Sibyls) requested a long life from Apollo who, on account of his love for her, had promised to fulfil her foremost desire. The sibyl neglected to also request eternal youthfulness. Apollo would only grant this in return for the her virginity. She refused, and so slowly grew old until she finally resembled a cicada and was suspended in a cage in the Temple of Apollo in Cuma.

Tiburtine Sibyl overlooking the Oval Fountain

Second Tiburtine Room, north wall, Athamas, driven mad by the Fury (right), murders his son Learchus while Ino flees with Melicertes

Second Tiburtine Room, soffit showing King Anio drowning as he tries to prevent his daughter from being carried away by Mercury; Below the cornice, Venus and Neptune, saviours of Ino and Melicertes, who are shown transformed into the water deities Leucothea and Palaemon

Second Tiburtine Room, soffit with Apollo, and below him, the Tiburtine Sibyl (Ino) and Melicertes as water deities, with river god Anio (surrounded by nine goats)

Second Tiburtine Room, northeast wall, journey of Tiburtine Sibyl (to or from Rome) and sacrifice of ram

Second Tiburtine Room, southwest wall, the Tiburtines and priests in praise of the sibyl

The Water Organ

The Water Organ, the Oval Fountain and the Rometta structure an intermediate level in the garden, marked by a path which recreates the legendary journey of the sibyl from the rocks below the Tiburtine Cascade to the Roman Campidoglio. This journey is first depicted as an illusion at the Water Organ (in a distant *sgraffito* scene of Rome painted on the wall adjacent to the apse of S Pietro della Carità), and then as an actual journey through the garden which begins at the Water Organ and arrives at the Rometta (an idealised model of antique Rome) via the Oval Fountain and the Line of a Hundred Fountains. The route follows an almost level path which overlooks the lower plateau of the garden.

Of all the arts, the Cardinal was particularly interested in the cultivation of antique music, and his court musician, *l'arcimusico* Nicola Vicentino, was noted for his practice of the art of ancient Greek music '*diatonico, cromatico ed enarmonico*'. The Cardinal funded Vicentino's publication, *L'Antica Musica Ridotta alla Moderna Prattica*, published in Rome in 1555. At the same time, the engineer Giovanni Battista Aleotti (who was responsible for the fountains at the Isola di Belvedere and the Giardini della Castellina in Ferrara) was part of the Estense circle, and it was his translation of Erone Alessandrino's *Pneumatica, Gli artifitiosi et curiosi moti spirituali di Herone*, published in Ferrara in 1589, which provided the key to rediscovering the ancient techniques of water-powered automata. To his translation of Erone, Aleotti added four theories of his own, the last of which describes a system of air-conditioning using the same technique of air supply as a hydraulic organ. The preciseness of the description, involving dimensions and careful instructions for waterproofing, indicates that the system was undoubtedly installed in the villa: Montaigne referred to 'large hollows underneath the palace' and to 'air holes which give out a cold vapour and impart a wonderful coolness to all the lower parts of the house'. Later Giovambattista della Porta described having seen Aleotti's cooling system:

I will recount a way of how we can still create a strong wind –
by making water fall through a channel into a chamber; and the
longer the channel, the stronger the wind. In the same way, in
the heat of the summer, we can cool rooms by circulating a strong
and fresh wind. This we have seen in Tivoli.[51]

The hydraulic organ at the Villa d'Este was begun by the Frenchman Luc Leclerc and completed by his nephew Claude Vernard (who had worked with him during the early stages). It was finished around 1569-72, in time for the visit of Pope Gregory III, who 'was so satisfied and admiring that he wanted to hear it twice and thrice again, and wanted to speak to M Claudio, its inventor'.[52] This description by Zappi, who was the first to describe the working organ in 1572, continued: 'Countless gentlemen could not believe that this organ played by itself, accord-

ing to the registers, with water; but they rather thought there was somebody inside'.[53] Audebert provided a detailed account of how the organ worked, describing a sealed underground chamber which generated the necessary air pressure.

The water supply from the Aniene was drawn directly from a large intake behind the Albunean Sibyl. It was channelled underneath the church of S Paolo della Carità, at which point it met a V-shaped iron gate high up behind the organ facade. The slow-flowing water passed either side of the gate, then the inflected base of the channel forced some water to flow back onto the gate, down the ceramic pipe and into the aeolic chamber. The water entering the chamber was aerated by the agitated flow around the gate and the movement down the staggered pipe.

The aeolic chamber was described as being beneath the rocky base for the statue of Diana of Ephesus, but in the present arrangement, perhaps as a result of extensive restorations, it is directly behind the statue. In the past, the chamber was typically half-filled with water. Two openings controlled the internal conditions; there was a window to indicate the water level, and a tap to relieve the pressure of the air above the water level. A third opening allowed the water to escape from below into the space of the niche of the fountain facade itself, and a fourth allowed the air to escape at high level through a pipe. The simple principle of the mechanism was that air and water entered together (as aerated water) into a controlled volume and then separated. The water was let out slowly to maintain the level, resulting in a build-up of air pressure above. At high pressure the air was allowed to escape, regulated to pass through the organ pipes. The water released out of the bottom of the chamber turned a wheel mechanism containing a musical score, which in turn operated a set of valves, opening and closing the pipes. The original invention was described by Audebert:

We enter, via a small portal, into a squared space – enclosed with
small walls. At the end of this is the Fountain of the Organ, which
surpasses all others, not for its richness but for its artifice and
ingenious secret. The fountain is more rustic than well decorated
– the lower part being like a rock – and at its base is a basin
shaped as three semicircles. Higher up, there is a modern stone
statue built as a herm representing 'Nature' – it is also called *La
Fontaine de la Nature*. The top part of the statue has a woman's
head without arms. The woman has a body covered by large
breasts resting one on top of the other; instead of legs, there is
a square tapered pillar finishing in a point.

Behind the statue pass twenty-two organ pipes corresponding to a small vaulted window which rises within a small vaulted opening. These pipes, without any human intervention, play music with all the scores as well as the finest musician. To make it more wonderful, the view of the mechanism is denied to visitors. However, I had the opportunity to have everything communicated to me and I went to the secret place where I curiously noticed all the movements and means of this admirable and ingenious invention which I will describe in accordance with what I have seen.

Under this rock-shaped structure of a fountain there is a small underground room vaulted like a cave, without any opening apart from the top. At a corner of the vault is a hole made large enough for a man to get through. To enter, one has to lift a big, square stone which closes this opening so precisely that air cannot get in or out. We climbed down into the room via this passage with a ladder. At one end of the room there is a big lead conduit which comes from the top, and at its extremity the water falls in abundance and with strength – the water falling in the room causes atmospheric agitation and generates wind.

The water is unable to find an outlet apart from a canal which is smaller than the one from the top, and not sufficient to reduce the quantity of water. The result is that a large amount of water stays in the room and, slowly, the volume of water rises and compresses the air. The canal into which the water falls is also linked to an iron wheel – with small paddles – similar to a water mill. The rotation of this wheel increases the wind, and sets in motion another iron wheel, similar to the previous one and of equal height – which means four or five feet from top to bottom – but narrower at about three feet wide.

A long strip covers the wheel: on top of it there are many small iron pieces heightened and welded to keep them straight. Some of them, longer, smaller or medium-sized, are used for the tempo: pause, long note, brief note, semi-brief, quaver, crotchet rest, and other things required for music.

At the top of the vault there are twenty-two small holes which line up with each organ pipe, but these are blocked by means of a small piece of tin applied over each hole and organ pipe. The piece of tin is no larger than a silver coin, and is cut into squares, hollowed in the middle so that the strength of the wind intensifies the pressure and keeps the hole blocked. Also, each tin piece is soldered to the end of a long iron stick which joins the wide wheel and almost touches it.

One of the ends is at a lower level, the other at a higher level, which is achieved by means of a second rod attached to the highest part of the vault. The vault keeps the rod suspended in equilibrium, having one side heavier than the other, and thus, one side is always close to the wheel, and on the other side, the tin always keeps the opening closed.

That is the arrangement . . . When the first wheel starts rotating, it makes the second one rotate and generates music (because of the bar, as has been said before). During the rotation, some of the teeth (raised and the height of one finger) touch the end

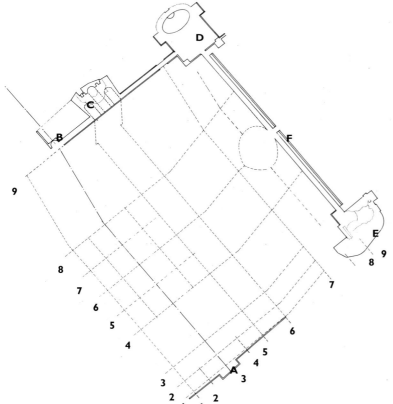

PAGES 62-63: Water Organ, Grottoes of the Sibyl with Bernini cascade, Neptune niche and modern water jets in foreground; PAGE 65: Schematic axonometric illustrating the Journey of the Sibyl, drawn by David Dernie (a) Fountain of Neptune (author's interpretation) (b) Fountain of Venus Cloacina (c) Grottoes of the Sibyl, Water Organ (d) Oval Fountain (e) Rometta (f) Line of a Hundred Fountains (principal paths across lower garden shown dotted)

Water Organ detail

Grotto of the Sibyl with opening to underground room – a resonance chamber (author's interpretation)

of the suspended iron stick, lifting it up. When the other end is at a lower level and the holes stay open, the wind is let through and the organ pipe resounds. The other teeth do the same, one after the other in accordance with their distribution on the wheel. The sound of the pipe lasts as long as there is wind inside; it varies along with the size of the tooth which touches the iron rod (brief or long).

That is the secret and the artifice of the fountain.[54]

Audebert continued, describing the continuous nightingale song which accompanied the five tunes of the organ's repertoire. His description accords with earliest records of payments dating from 1567-68, and confirms the original arrangement of the statue of Diana of Ephesus above a miniature mountain (monticello) representing, according to Cartari, a symbol of the 'hidden virtue' of the earth, an:

omnipotent god, Natura Naturante, which creates and nurtures all the heavenly and earthly things and is the Virtù which gives itself to the cause seconde, through which the universe is generated and governed.

In this context, the statue of Diana of Ephesus must also allude to the sibyl herself: after Leucothea had been washed ashore on the banks of the Tiber, the prophetess Carmenta had foretold that her fate was to be celebrated as Mater Matuta.

In 1582, the organ was vandalised by a local in search of tin (Cardinal Luigi d'Este took pity on the culprit: instead of punishing him, he gave him five hundred gold florins), and it fell into ruin when the villa was abandoned after the death of Luigi in 1586. The statues of Apollo and Orpheus now seen flanking the central aedicule, together with the reliefs of Apollo and Orpheus above the cornice line, the snake-limbed caryatids, the two Victories and the eagle surmounting the organ, were all part of the restorations under Alessandro d'Este between 1609-15. Bernini altered the cascade in 1661, and finally, in 1927, the current arrangement of fountains in front of the organ was constructed. This dramatically altered its original character, but such was the enthusiasm for these new fountains that one of the images of the organ in the Salotto was overpainted to illustrate the alteration (see p70).

A second fresco dating from 1568-69 survives, and illustrates the organ against the backdrop of the town. It appears as if in a garden clearing (see p71), and is shown enclosed with a circular screen which is open towards the front, and flanked on either side by herms 'to illustrate nature', according to Audebert. The Du Pérac legend describes Apollo and Diana in the niches between the herms, but all other documents support the fresco. Audebert offered this description of the Deluge:

... Because of the noise made by the strength and force of the water, there appears to be a tempest or a storm. The water coming up from underground thrusts up into the sky to a height of two spears. At the end of the tempest it dies down and

flows slowly and ordinarily: this is what they call Le Deluge. In the middle of the water, there is a rock triton holding a trumpet, which resonates with a hoarse sound during the tempest and the storm. The sound starts first with a whispering and slowly increases in intensity. Dying down at the end, it makes a gurgling and murmuring which seem to come from far away, as if the triton was gone.[55]

Before the alterations by Bernini in 1661, the facade of the organ below the terrace level was much less articulated. Built deep into the supporting wall, the three grottoes – illustrated in the Salotto fresco and 'dedicated to the sibyls to honour most highly the Tiburtine Sibyl'[56] – are intriguing, for they bring together at least two important illusions. First, the sibyl overlooks the lower garden and with musical voice foretells the apocalyptic flood, and the 'voices of many animals and sounds of almost every instrument beautiful and musical'.[57] Not only was Ino the daughter of Cadmus and Harmony, but the oracular power of the 'Fonte Albunea' was related to notes, or sounds; Ligorio, for instance, quoted the Aeneid (Bk7): 'Lucosque sub alta consulit Albunea, nemorum quae maxima sacro fonte sonat'. Second, the tumultuous noise evoked the Valle d'Inferno where, according to legend, the Tiburtine Sibyl was found and lifted up to the Acropolis, where the circular temple (the original circular screen) was consecrated to her.[58] The Water Organ not only alluded to the musical Albunea spring, but appeared as a model of the Tiburtine Cascade: similar to the model of antique Rome constructed at the Fountain of the Rometta on the other side of the garden.

The ingenious arrangement, whereby the sibyl's prophecies appeared to emerge from the earth as partially articulated music, depended on the presence of a little-known room behind the two basins of her fountain niche. Barely visible, behind the screen of water in the back wall (which is over three metres thick), is a crude, narrow opening that seems to have been carved out by water. This opens into a mysterious room, four metres square in plan, with a barrel-vaulted ceiling two-and-a-half metres off the floor at the highest point. The room is animated by a pale light and flickering shadows as the afternoon sun passes through the water of the cascade. From the floor of roughly hewn travertine grows a circular travertine stone embedded in an otherwise unarticulated rear wall. The irregular niche is aligned with the opening to the Grotto of the Sibyl, and it seems likely that this was connected by a vertical pipe to the organ itself. The piped music of the organ would have reverberated in the chamber, creating the illusion of sounds emanating from deep within the earth. From the sibyl's grotto, the voice of the prophetess would have been part-music, part-water; these semi-articulated sounds, seemingly latent in the Aniene water itself, were her divinely inspired words. The foretold Apocalyptic Flood was represented by the thunderous sound of the water as it cascaded between the two basins in her grotto. The design of this fountain is similar to that of the fountain behind Noah's Ark, in the scene of the Flood painted by Muziano in the vaulted entrance to the courtyard of the villa.[59]

The Water Organ in its original state must have been spectacular: the upper portion of its west-facing facade was a resplendent wall of marble, glass, gold and mirror mosaic, gathering a domain of light and harmonious music; below, were dark generative caves filled with half-formed sounds. The musical Water Organ was ingeniously manipulated to create the illusion of a continuity between light and dark, heaven and earth. The sun-filled space of the organ gave out the heavenly music of Apollo. Like the sun's warm rays, it was reflected on earth, inspiring the arts, the music of Orpheus, and the sibyl's prophecies.

From her cave below the Tiburtine Cascade, the sibyl was lifted up to her temple and carried to Rome. The original circular screen at the heart of the organ's facade alluded to the circular temple, and to underline the idea of the journey, an image of Rome as a distant city was drawn in *sgraffito* on the adjoining apse wall of S Paolo della Carità. The illusionistic scene included seats painted to look like porphyry, and false windows looking out onto a mountain landscape: between 'the Fountain of the Organ and the House of S Peter (Church of S Pietro della Carità) were works in *sgraffito*, that is Rome, made all in *sgraffito* and painting, simulacra and letters'.[60] Like a mirror, the painted wall represented a distant Rome and the garden's Rometta.

In the same way that the Rometta was a summary of the sibyl's journey in itself (being a model of both Tivoli and Rome), so the Water Organ represented the sibyl's Tiburtine cave and combined this illusion with a painting of distant Rome and a statue of Romulus and Remus which was also in her grotto.[61] It was characteristic that these settings, while being part of a journey, were also summaries of the entire journey, offering enough visual references to furnish the learned observer with a broader picture.

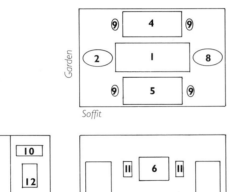

Soffit

 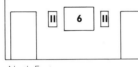 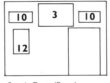 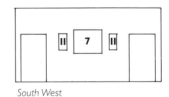

North West (Garden) *North East* *South East (Rear)* *South West*

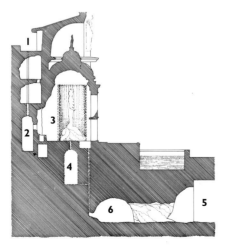

ABOVE: Second Tiburtine Room, drawn by David Dernie (1) Apollo the sun god (2) Athamas murders Learchus (3) Venus and Neptune, saviours of Ino and Melicertes who are transformed into the water deities Leucothea and Palaemon (4) the rivers Tiber, Anio and Erculaneo (5) Tiburtine Sibyl at the mouth of the Tiber (6) Journey of the Sibyl, Tiburtines offer a sacrifice of a ram (7) Adoration of the Sibyl, her Tiburtine temple in the background (8) King Anio is drowned pursuing Cloris (9) Personifications of music and drama (10) Ceres' search for Proserpina (11) landscapes; BELOW: Section through Water Organ and Grotto of the Sibyl as existing, based on a survey by the Soprintendenza per i Beni Ambientali e Architettonici del Lazio (1) water and air intake (2) aeolic chamber (3) original location of Diana of Ephesus and circular screen (4) location of aeolic chamber according to Audebert, author's interpretation (5) Grotto of Tiburtine Sibyl (6) square room, the purpose of which may have been to resonate piped music or the sounds of water when released from the aeolic chamber

Salotto, northwest wall detail, fresco of Water Organ repainted to show actual arrangement

Salotto, northwest wall fresco, detail showing original circular screen, herms and grottoes below

The Oval Fountain

The Oval Fountain is like a fulcrum between the Water Organ and the Rometta. If at the Water Organ the sibyl appears as the Goddess of Nature, at the Oval Fountain she becomes Mnemosyne, mother of the Muses. In this new guise, she appears with Melicertes in a cave at the base of an artificial hill – a recreation of Mount Helicon.

Foglietta gave an elaborate description of the Oval Fountain since, 'it has already been completed, whereas the others have not yet been fully executed':

> it consists of a mound, the crest of which does not stretch gradually, but is distinguished by several peaks of unequal heights. The mount forms a bent shape, which is referred to as oval. It comprises monstrous projecting stones of the kind formed by the ceaseless discharge of water emerging from the rock; they are not dissimilar to dripstones, and in colour, close to pumice stone. These are treated in such an artistic manner and the rising masses of the large stones are ordered so artificially that the whole is pleasing to the visitor, although they evoke a raw and awesome impression like a natural mountain. On the lower part of the mound three caves are excavated. In the central one, there is the image of a woman sitting on a chair; in the right and left ones, there are reclining figures of rivers, all on a colossal scale.

Out of the caves, the water gushes into three basins situated below the figures, and then flows down continuously, contained partly by a straight masonry canal and partly by two narrow *euripi*. These accompany the half circle of the raised pergola whose curves eventually conduct the water into a large basin resting on a very strong column. The pergola is secured by a parapet of small columns. A large volume of water overflows continuously all around it and out of the basin, pouring down into a spacious, oval-shaped pool. The noise of the water is such that one can barely hear the voices of people standing nearby. A marble ball rises up from the centre of the pool, onto which are affixed four upturned lead ducts. Three [of them] describe a triangle, the fourth is in its centre. Water jets rise out of them and then fall in an arc so that they express a beautiful form similar to lily blossom.

The place benefits considerably from the plane trees which stand around the square and darken it with agreeable shade. Above all, the sublimity of the place is increased by a grotto to the left of the square, the wall niches of which are decorated and ordered beautifully with statues of excellent workmanship and great value, and are furthermore decorated with paintings and marble crowns and dice work. This grotto serves as a lounge (*praebet ad hexedrae usum*) in the heat of the summer. Its natural situation alone offers refreshment, since it is of course largely

driven into the ground by soil and rocks. The sound of the cascading water outside and the murmuring of the well inside delights the ear . . . Here, the welcome afternoon sessions take place.

. . . Out of the three wells in the Tiburtine region spring three rivers, which water Tibur's borders and which then reunite and eventually flow into the Tiber: the Anio, of a famous name, the Erculaneo and the Albunea . . . The lower water pool represents the sea which the three rivers and the Tiber flow out into.

Foglietta does not mention the travertine statue of Pegasus which leaps from the summit of this mountain of dripstone over a second smaller oval basin. The winged horse identifies the fountain with Mount Helicon, '*monte piantato di Lauri del Cavallo Pegaso*', the home of the Muses and source of the divinely inspired arts.[62] Its head is tilted towards the villa as though in recognition of Cardinal Ippolito d'Este's patronage of the arts and sciences. The Cardinal was like Apollo – the light of the sun, the source of all inspiration (the same epithet was attached to the Medici Pope Leo X, who in 1517 was heralded as a new Apollo, making the Vatican Hill a new Parnassus).[63]

The appearance of the fountain today is somewhat deceptive, for, like much of the rest of the garden, its court has been paved. Originally, the ground surfaces of the garden's pathways and external enclosures were mostly finished in terracotta, and, as archive images show, the Oval Fountain had a grove-like quality and was heavily shaded by ten plane trees. Ligorio's description of Mount Helicon as 'the dark and shaded grove of the Muses', could allude to the fountain itself in its original state. Ligorio did not mention laurel trees in his description, but as leader of the Muses, Apollo was often depicted with a laurel-wreath crown. Laurel trees were planted at a high level at the Oval Fountain, along the Line of a Hundred Fountains and on either side of the path to the Water Organ (after 1611, Apollo's statue stood on one side of the travertine Diana of Ephesus, with Orpheus on the other side).

A possible further reference to the Muses (plus Apollo) lies in the ten statues of peperino stone which are housed in the niches of the fountain's arcaded wall. Foglietta called them Nereids, sea nymphs and daughters of Nereus, the 'old man of the sea' in Greek mythology, underlining his assertion that the oval basin represented the sea.

Ligorio's description of Mount Helicon continued, 'the cave of the nymphs (Muses), was placed on one of the elm-covered banks of the River Helicon'. At the Villa d'Este, the only elm-covered banks (elm being one of the three woods of Christ's cross) were those rising above the Line of a Hundred Fountains, and the only cave in that bank was the Grotto of Diana. Ligorio hinted at the idea of a fragmented Mount Parnassus:

> Over the waters of the fountain, which came from the cave, were the horse Pegasus, who was mirrored in the violet water, and the

images of Orpheus [legendary poet skilled with lyre] and Calliope [inventor of Poetry], who stood apart from but near the other Muses.[64]

Perhaps the allusion to a new Parnassus extended beyond the enclosure of the Oval Fountain to encompass the Grotto of Diana (the cave of the nymphs) and the Water Organ (the celebration of the art of music). This would provide an explanation for the presence of Minerva in the Grotto of Diana. Whilst the principal niche in this grotto, that of Diana, faced out towards the garden, a statue of Minerva occupied a second niche, facing towards the west, where a vaulted opening gave views over the valley below. Minerva may have been the first figure encountered by the Cardinal's guests as they descended to the garden down the spiral stair that connected the dining terrace to the grotto. Minerva was commonly associated with wisdom and memory, but also, in Ovid's *Metamorphoses*,[65] with the Muses, and Cartari records that Minerva was called 'Goddess of Wisdom and inventor of all the arts'.[66]

Finally, it is useful to refer to the iconography of Ligorio's decoration at the Casino of Pius IV, where the facade of the loggia facing the courtyard has a stucco frieze depicting the Muses led in dance by Apollo. Opposite is the two-storey facade of the Casino itself, with a central image which Smith interprets as an alabaster vase representing the source of Truth and of the Hours, the contents of which are poured onto the *cortile* below. Like the Casino, the Oval Fountain at Tivoli has centred over it a large, chalice-like, mosaic-covered urn which pours water from the Castalian spring. A thin film of water, reflecting the glistening white mosaic surface of the vase, flows ceaselessly into the fish-filled basin (ocean) as if representing the body of truth flowing from the sibyl.[67] The sibyl now becomes Mnemosyne – mother of the

Muses and personification of Truth. On one occasion Ligorio associated Mnemosyne with the Castalian spring and described her as carrying a flowing urn:

> The poets say that Memory is a divine thing and the mother of the Muses. Perhaps for this reason, she has the cithara of Apollo and an urn pouring water, an imitation of the fountain sacred to her daughters in Castilia, the place of both the chorus of the Muses and of their cave and temple.[68]

The central support to the marble basin of the Oval Fountain is finished in white mosaic. At its centre is a marble ball, out of which spurt four water jets forming the shape of a fleur-de-lys. This resembles the marble mosaic fountain in the background of the stucco relief of Pan and Syrinx in the Grotto of Diana. The nine white birds of the mosaic fly from the basin: like the nine birds in Muziano's Salotto fresco, they refer to the sibyl's divinely inspired prophecies. At the Oval Fountain, the image of the allegorical birds resembles the delicately thin veil of white water which constantly flows from the basin. The column-base of the basin is finished in white mosaic, the fragmented surface of which dissolves as the lines between material elements and ripples in the water merge to create an image which is as much part of the water as it is of the fountain structure. The upper basin of this structure resembles a chalice (as the symbolic vessel of the prophetic word, the earth's globe at the centre) and it seems to float above the ocean, presenting the image of a splitting shell: the symbolic separation of heaven and earth. What connects these two features are the divinely inspired words of the sibyl, represented here as a delicate veil of water, against a light and glistening mosaic.

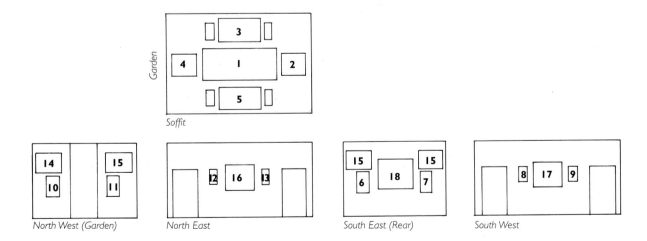

First Tiburtine Room, drawing by David Dernie (1) landing of Tivoli's legendary founders at Latium (2) augury scene with thunderbolt (3) sacrifice with Tiburtus ploughing to define city walls (4) building the town (5) building with the Temple of the Sibyl in background (6) Jupiter (7) Juno (8) Apollo (9) Diana (10) Bacchus (11) Ceres (12) Vulcan (13) Venus with Cupid (14) Oval Fountain under construction (15) landscapes (16) founding brothers in battle against the Sicani (17) sacrifice after victory (18) Hercules Saxanus

Oval Fountain, Tiburtine Sibyl with Melicertes flanked by two river gods. Ten nymphs and Venus born from a shell can be seen below

Pegasus and the Fountain of Hippocrene

Salotto, southeast wall fresco, detail showing Oval Fountain

Oval Fountain detail

Oval Fountain, detail showing Venus born from a shell

Oval Fountain, detail of passage behind oval pool

The Grotto of Venus and the Fountains of Bacchus

Two further fountains are located in the walled enclosure of the Oval Fountain, within the paired niches dedicated to Bacchus and the Grotto of Venus. Both Bacchus and Venus feature in the legend of the Tiburtine Sibyl; Venus and the oval basin refer to the sea and to the transformation of Ino into Leucothea. Bacchus was fostered by Ino after his mother Semele perished at the sight of Jupiter. Like Jupiter, Bacchus was also nurtured by the nymphs of grottoes and mountains, and has a paired niche probably to refer to his being twice born, as indeed Ino was twice saved. Furthermore, as Smith points out, Ligorio occasionally identified Bacchus as leader of the Muses, 'The antiques made Bacchus leader of the Muses, like Apollo, and he was called Musagete and Philochro among the poets who wrote that Bacchus was nurtured by the Muses'.

According to the Du Pérac legend, the Grotto of Venus was dedicated to 'voluptuous pleasure', contrasting with the chaste Diana's Grotto, and this relationship has been interpreted as part of a primary theme, concerning virtue and vice, which may have conditioned the general layout of the garden. The choice that the youthful Hercules had to make between virtue and his lustful stepmother, Phaedra, is symbolised by the Pythagorean 'Y', reflected in the garden by the divergent paths beyond the Fountain of the Dragon.

Some aspects of this interpretation are less than convincing. For instance, why should the Grotto of Venus, if it is associated so strongly with voluptuous pleasure, be located within the enclosure of the fountain specifically relating to Tivoli, its founding, its glorification as a new Parnassus and abode of the Tiburtine Sibyl? The presence of at least six other statues of Venus (one in the *cortile*, one in the Cardinal's private apartments, one in the Salotto and three in the garden) implies that Venus had a more complex meaning. In Ligorio's words:

> There is a difference between one Venus and the other because the first is Universal Mother of all things and she is the beautiful, heavenly Venus. The other is the *terrestre*, who operates here down on earth, mother of all loves and all intelligences of all things, and in harmony with heavenly Venus. The third is mother of Cupid, ugly and armed with bows and arrows, and she represents the lustful and horrible actions of mortals.[69]

The divine *anima* is manifest in beauty, and love is the desire of that beauty.[70] The three forms of Venus described by Ligorio reflect the two aspects of Venus common to Neo-Platonic thought – 'Venus Coelestis' or celestial Venus, goddess of contemplative love, and 'Venus Vulgaris', goddess of beauty in the corporeal world and of active love, whose origin is in Plato's *Symposium* – plus a third aspect representing the desire for sensual pleasure,[71] 'bestial love', and the abandonment of a contemplative life. It is possible that the three rooms planned for the Grotto

of Venus were to refer to this understanding of the iconography, but the grotto was never completed as planned. Sometime before 1611, Venus was replaced with a statue of Bacchus, but originally she stood on a rock in a central niche between a set of three smaller niches, each of which housed a tartaro rock. Below her were four *putti* which poured water into a basin.

The spirit of love which Venus represents is a mediating link between the invisible and infinite love of God and the physical love of human life. Love, as a central theme of Neo-Platonic philosophy – from Ficino, Pico della Mirandola to, in the sixteenth century, Leone Ebreo – is the means by which God causes himself to be infused in the world. As such, both the Venus Grotto at the Oval Fountain, and the Fountain of Venus Cloacina to the north of the Water Organ (mentioned by Du Pérac and Audebert) frame the eastern stretch of the middle horizon and are analogous to the pair of fountains on the garden's western edge dedicated to Minerva, inventor of the arts. As fountains dedicated to Love and Knowledge, they flank the Fountain of the Dragon, representing dual symmetrical themes which structure the east and west boundaries. Both of these sequences find a complement in a fountain above the level of the Line of a Hundred Fountains, as though to convey the message that a life dedicated to Love and Knowledge of God would open the path beyond the lower garden to the virtuous domain of the Cardinal (see p87).

That these two themes are related in this way is implied in the internal geometrical order of the garden with a straight line that joins the Grotto of Venus, the Jupiter niche, and the Fountain of the Owls, the chief attribute of Minerva (see plan p9).

OPPOSITE: Cartari, Neptune in horse-drawn chariot with Amphitrite. The waves represent the sea and Venus; the figure sitting on the dolphin is Palaemon, god of the ports. This image relates Venus to Melicertes and the sea, which is the appellation Foglietta gives the basin at the Oval Fountain; ABOVE: Grotto of Venus (statue replaced)

Fountain of the Owls towards west

The Fountain of the Owls

The Fountain of the Owls was begun around 1565 and finished in 1569 by the Frenchman Luc Leclerc, who went on to build the Water Organ. The theme was a traditional one: a cycle in which singing birds would hush upon the sight of an approaching owl and then once more begin to chatter when out of danger. This naturalistic movement — and at Tivoli it was said to be so refined that when the birds began to sing they started up timidly — was created artificially, using ancient techniques very similar in principle to those described for the Water Organ. The fountain attracted much attention and is here described at length by Audebert:

> On this one there is a boar's head which comes out of the wall and around it are three naked men who seem to hold it still. Two of them, seated beside, are holding it by the neck, the other is behind helping them.
>
> A fountain, which flows from the boar's snout into a basin below, is held up by three satyrs. On both sides of the statues and the boar, under the vault, there are four large olive tree branches (they are an imitation, made of painted iron), over which there are twenty little birds made of bronze, each one painted according to its real colour. These birds sing in a varied manner, the artifice reproducing real singing. However, between one of the statue's feet and the boar's snout, an owl appears slowly. As soon as it withdraws and disappears, the birds start to sing again. They do not sing immediately and simultaneously but only one starts the twittering of a chaffinch, then another one murmurs a continuous and low twitter, as if scared of what it has seen; a third also starts to twitter, and then gathered together, they begin to sing as before and continue until the owl returns.
>
> The way this is done is as follows: there are a number of little whistles, like the ones used by bird-catchers to imitate the singing of birds. The whistles are linked to a canal which is filled with wind by means of water, so that each of the whistles produces a sound. When the owl appears it is first in a position where it suddenly blocks the conduit pipe connected to the chaffinch. Withdrawing further, it allows the wind to enter another whistle, which twitters gently, since there is not enough wind. Finally, the same thing happens with another whistle, then when the owl has completely disappeared and all the conduits are open, all the birds start to sing loudly in an uncoordinated way, creating a sound similar to that experienced when one first enters an aviary.

The fountain forms part of a sequence of garden rooms — enclosed spaces open to the sky — on the southwestern edge of the garden. Arriving in the piazza of the Rometta, a paired staircase works around a double wall which forms the edge of the fountain that was dedicated in the seventeenth century to Proserpine (but was originally intended to be the Fountain of the Emperors, dedicated to four Emperors associated with Tivoli — Augustus, Trajan, Hadrian and Caesar). This opens onto a second room, the Fountain of the Owls, which is enclosed on four sides by a high wall articulated with pilasters and containing niches with seats to watch the spectacle. After the death of Cardinal Ippolito, Alessandro d'Este had the walls of the room painted to complete the iconographic programme. Del Re described the painting when three of the walls were complete:

> In one of these niches, the carriage of the Sun is painted at the top, and at the bottom, a scene of a quail hunt, fields of wheat and other summer things. On another, in front of the previous one, is an image of Fetonte who, frightened by the sign of the scorpion in the zodiac, falls from his father's carriage. Below is a bird-catcher enticing thrushes with a whistle . . . and the usual hunting scenes of autumn. In another part is depicted the burial of Fetonte attended by his crying sisters, who transform him into trees on the banks of the river Eridano, today called Pò. In another niche is painted Icarus and his father flying, and then Icarus, with wings melted by the sun, falling into the sea, which is named after him. The fourth niche is not yet painted. On the upper part of the two walls facing north are painted scenes of hunters mending and making nets and cages . . . On the opposite side are painted transformations of men and women into birds, as described in Ovid's *Metamorphoses*.[72]

It is from Minerva's attribute of the owl that the fountain takes its name, and like Minerva, Icarus' father Daedalus represented the inventiveness of the human mind. Ovid's *Metamorphoses* (8:183-235) recounts that in order to escape from imprisonment on Crete, Daedalus constructed pairs of wings for his son and himself: 'Take care to fly a middle course,' he warned, 'if you sink too low, the waves may weight your feathers; if too high, the heat will burn them'. But as Icarus began to enjoy his flight, he forgot his father's guidance and soared too high. The sun melted his wings of fragrant wax and he perished in the waves below. The fall of Icarus symbolised the limits of human invention and spoke of the eternal quest of the artist to create like nature. On the opposite wall of the open room enclosing the fountain were scenes depicting the fruits of natural creativity, ordered according to the seasons.

The creativity of the artist-genius was reflected by the ingenious automata, with its artificial bronze birds which sang and flew from the approaching owl. As if to warn of the limits of human invention, the scene was played against the backdrop of a mountain of watery tartaro, constantly in shadow, as a symbol of the generative earth — and the fruits of that mysterious process were painted on the fountain's walls. More subtle was the play across the garden to the Grotto of Venus, an embodiment of natural creativity: the two fountains were linked by a straight line passing through the Jupiter niche at the Fountain of the Dragon. Lucretius dedicated his *De Rerum Natura* to Venus, as 'genetrix', whom he called the creative power of Nature itself, since love and desire are the source of all life:

> Mother of Romans (Venus, mother of Encas and progenitor of the Romans), lustful pleasure of men and gods: *Venere Nutrice*, for you the stars wandering in the skies, the seas carrying ships, the fields fertile with wheat and full of creatures. Only for you every kind of living creature can be conceived and as soon as they emerge out of darkness they can see the light of the sun.[73]

Venus and Proserpina together share the love of Adonis in a legend identified with the hidden generative spirit of the earth:

> Proserpina is the soul which flows in earthly substances and is the same as psyche. That is, she is the *anima* that comes from the depths of the earth and brings forth flowers, and on account of its heavenly *virtù*, produces fruit.[74]

The dedication of the fountain to Proserpina allowed the relationship between nature's creativity, and the inventiveness of the human mind (the automata of the Fountain of the Owls) to be visually combined within the two open rooms, and then reiterated in the subject-matter of the frescoes. The connection was also made geometrically and as a journey from the Grotto of Venus. This link was part of a broader theme in the garden involving an analogy between two sequences of grottoes; one related to Venus, working up the garden's eastern edge, and the other related to Minerva, commencing with the Fountain of the Owls on the western boundary. The earlier dedication of the fountain to the Emperors articulated the orientation of human wisdom towards the contemplation and admiration of history, and specifically, Tiburtine history. In the original (never completed) arrangement, the niche of the Emperors' Fountain was framed by Salomonic columns.

The analogy between natural and human creativity is perhaps best understood by referring to Federico Zucarro, whose treatise *L'idea de' pittori scultori ed architetti* (1607) described the human faculty of *disegno* (design in its fullest sense) as 'almost another sun, another generative nature'. At the same time, the image of Icarus perishing as he flies too close to the sun is a reminder that although man is 'almost a second god', the products of his creativity can only aspire to the perfection of the divine mind: 'The difference between the art of God, producing natural things, and our art, producing artificial things, is that the former is more perfect, pervasive and of infinite virtue, and these are conditions which our art lacks'.[75]

One particularly influential text was Erone Alessandrino's *Automata e Pneumatica*, translated and published with an introduction by Bernardino Baldi in 1589, which illustrated a fountain similar to the Fountain of the Owls. What Baldi referred to as '*il principio interno del moto* (the internal principle of movement)', created by the mathematics of the artificer, seemed to supersede Ficino's definition of art as a 'nature which models material from the outside'. Artists now appeared to be able to create like nature itself. Their machines transformed water into song and flight and operated almost like magic; the movement implied an internal force which alluded to the creative spirit of nature and was analogous to the movement of the soul.

Movement was inherent in this conception of nature's creativity, as underlined by Lucretius' proposal that a void could not exist. The continual motion of the four elements was understood to be the cause of all things, a notion which inspired Buontalenti to investigate perpetual motion in the Florentine court of Francesco I. In the words of Salomon de Caus, 'We know nothing of emptiness'[79] – that is, water moves in the earth to maintain the lack of a void. But the space of the Mannerist grotto and the opening of the earth created a void which revealed the mysterious 'internal creative principle' represented in the movement of water and the growth of living stone. The grotto wall can be described as emblematic of the creative spirit (*anima*) of the earth.

Thus the human intellect mirrored the creativity of nature and, like the fruits of the earth, made visible the hidden process that emanated from God. Hence, the fascination with automata in the late Renaissance was not a purely scientific pursuit, but part of a much broader issue concerned with the relationship between art and nature and, more specifically, with the tendency which equated the artificial with the divine: to create as artificially as possible came to be equated with the highest form of worship, for the artificial work of art celebrated the God-given genius of the artist and made it visible for all to admire.

It is not surprising to find that so much of the garden is highly artificial in character – from its miniature landscapes to its painted and stuccoed surfaces. Stucco is inherently false or artificial; it is at once highly workable and capable of being moulded into the most expressive surfaces. Whilst having a stone-like surface (Vasari describes how lime paste is mixed with the dust of stones and marbles), it has a fluidity which allows it to be imprinted with the *disegno* using moulding or imprinting techniques. It is often referred to as *stucco finto* (artificial stucco) since it is a kind of artificially created 'stone', but working it is very different to sculpting a piece of stone or marble to create naturalistic surfaces. In stuccowork, the human *disegno* takes part in the very creation of the 'stone' itself. Del Re marvelled at the statues of the ten nymphs, first carved in peperino stone and then stuccoed, for they were like stone, but stone created by the artist. As such, they reflected the *ingenium* of the artist who gained inspiration from the divine mind, the source of all beauty and harmony on the earth.

Zuccaro described the *disegno* as *forma*, meaning that it contains the light of the intellect. Angels are described as being of *forma* alone, while other beings are of *forma* and material. The less material obstructing the God-given idea, the greater the virtue displayed in the work. The tendency to stucco even the most admired of stones (including peperino and travertine) is related to this notion of the 'dematerialised' idea being closer to revealing the divine light of the artist's genius. The fineness of stucco paste, its ability to be moulded, painted and carved, means that it reveals none of the natural figuration inherent in stone or brick. It is close to the skies; it simply represents the *Idea*.

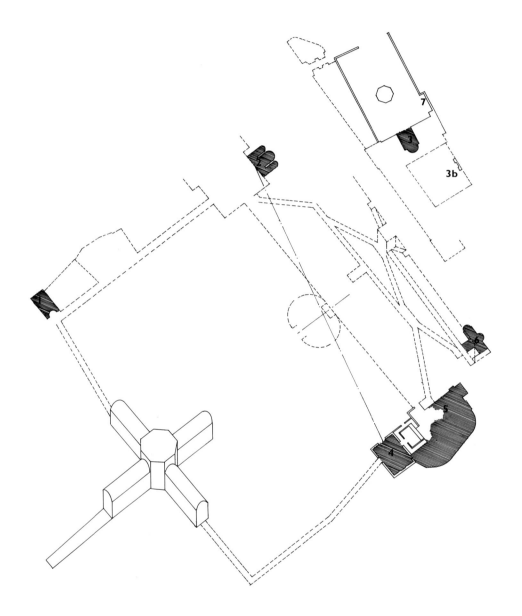

Schematic axonometric showing paths through Minerva and Venus fountains, drawing by David Dernie (1) Venus Cloacina (2) Venus Grotto (3) Grotto of Sleeping Venus (3b) Fountain of Venus (surmounted with a bust of Constantine) (4) Fountain of the Owls (5) Rometta, statue of Minerva (Roma) (6) Grotto of Diana and Minerva (7) Fountain of the Unicorn in secret garden. Note alignment of (2) and (4) through the Jupiter niche at the Fountain of the Dragon

Rometta towards the Tiburtine Cascade and statue of Appennino

The Rometta

Begun in 1567-68, the Rometta sits at the western end of the Line of a Hundred Fountains and, like the Oval Fountain, was almost certainly designed by Ligorio. It is set in part on a curved, raised platform, built out beyond the line of the existing city walls to provide an impressive brick and stucco model of antique Rome as seen from Trastevere.[76]

The space of this oval promontory is structured by a range of part-architectural, part-garden elements: stairs, retaining walls, sculptural figures, planted slopes and, at the southern edge, a mass of tartaro. All of these combine to give the space an ambiguous theatre-like character, and its paved surface undoubtedly provided a setting for a diverse range of performances, from sacred festivals to mimes and firework displays. The theatrical performances organised for the Cardinal's arrival in Rome in 1549 are well known, as are the tragedies written by Muret and recited in the Cardinal's court. Of particular interest, too, are the temporary theatrical settings that were often constructed in the gardens for banquets and summer dining.

To the left of the entrance from the Line of a Hundred Fountains is a small fountain oriented towards the sunset. The central portion of its facade comprises a series of ten diagonal channels which criss-cross against a background of stucco encrusted with exotic shells. Two gentle streams of water lace back and forth down the facade and into a square antique marble basin carved with reliefs of men and animals in battle. Next follows a low basin, faced with fragments of antique friezes plundered from Hadrian's Villa. Among these was a relief of Hercules and his Tiburtine Temple. A stepped bridge provided a way across the curved basin to a raised lawn. Here, Del Re described a satirical scene:

> Under a grotto sits a countrywoman tending hens; on the same
> lawn are two goat-herders, one leaning on a stick with a dog by
> his side, and the other with his trousers down relieving himself.
> They look at two goats butting.[77]

The southern edge of this area, the head of the fountain, is formed by an artificial cliff made of large pieces of tartaro on a brick substructure. Like the stone of which the fountain is made – *pietra tiburtina* – this represents the surrounding landscape with the Tiburtine Acropolis at its summit. Here, a giant statue of a reclining river god, Aniene, embraces the circular temple of the Tiburtine Sibyl. In his right hand he holds a cornucopia, symbol of the nutritive waters crashing down the face of the rocks below, recreating the famous Tiburtine Cascade. At the foot of the cascade is a cave, perhaps representing the actual Grotto of Neptune. In it is a giant figure of Apennino which supports the cliff. According to Del Re, there were two further figures representing the Erculaneo and the Tiber, 'King of all the Rivers'. These two rivers unite and flow across the curved face of the Rometta platform itself to meet an is-

land, in the form of a boat, which represents the Tiber island, S Bartolomeo. A stone obelisk rises from the centre of the boat, together with a coiled serpent representing Aesculapius and an eagle representing Jupiter. In antiquity there were temples to both gods on the boat-shaped island.

To the right of the boat is a bridge giving access to the upper platform, which Del Re described as a piazza or *teatro semiovato*. Along the top edge of the retaining wall for this level was a series of ten jets of water which fell into the Tiber below. Several other jets of water were hidden around the fountain, in seats, stairs, and by the gate on the bridge – these were activated by an unsuspecting visitor treading or sitting on a particular spot, and were carefully designed to soak 'from the waist down'.

On this level of the fountain was the famous model of antique Rome. Built in seven parts, it contained seven celebrated buildings which symbolised the seven hills of Rome as viewed from the Janiculum Hill. The idealised view of the city had at its centre the Campidoglio – the same point of view, as Maria Luisa Madonna has pointed out, that Ligorio assumed for his plan of Rome of 1561.[78] In front of the Campidoglio was a travertine statue personifying Rome; however, with an upright spear in her right hand, she bore more of a resemblance to Minerva and referred to the porphyry statue of Minerva in the actual Campidoglio. To one side, were statues representing the twin brothers Romulus and Remus being suckled by a wolf, and to the other, was a pedestal surmounted by a statue of a lion tearing a horse apart with its teeth and claws – a well-known image representing the battle between the peoples of Rome and Tivoli. The horse (Tivoli) loses the battle and so remains under Roman rule. In addition, there were two small statues in white marble; one showing Mercury, the other Bacchus holding a glass overflowing with grapes.

Despite the Cardinal's interest in theatre, it would be a mistake to consider the Rometta as solely a monumental backdrop for performance. Its significance is more complex. Synthesising Ligorio's vast archaeological knowledge of Roman topography, it is a built version of numerous reconstructions of antique buildings, an expression of the value placed on the cultivation of memory and its role in creating the new golden age. It is an idealised city, a paradigm for the future. As such, it can be seen as a vehicle for learned discourse, a kind of 'memory theatre', where erudite visitors to the garden could be reminded of the rich legends of ancient Rome and Tivoli. In this respect, it is interesting to read the account of Del Re who, after identifying each subject, was then diverted at length into accounts of the legends associated with it.

The significance of the Rometta is twofold. First, it concludes the allegorical journey around the garden from the Water Organ, via the Oval Fountain (Tivoli), to Rome itself, and thus defines the middle horizon of the garden. At the centre of its seven hills is the Capitoline and a model of the Campidoglio, where the sibyl offered an explanation of the priest's dreams; the sibylline texts were stored in the Temple of Jupiter, symbolised by the eagle sitting in the boat-island. Second, the Rometta replays the themes of the garden as if in summary. It has a dominant horizon, like the garden itself, and its lower entrance level is overshadowed by a miniature Tiburtine Cascade. Raised slightly above the entrance level, facing the Campidoglio scene, is a small fountain with a facade comprising ten diagonal intersecting channels. This represents the garden above the Line of a Hundred Fountains, which is characterised by a series of diagonal paths. The two streams of the fountain resemble the two sources of water for the upper garden (the Rivellese and rainwater); also represented are the birds of the Muziano fresco, and the ten apples on the intertwined branches forming the Cardinal's

impresa, which refer to the upper garden as a paradise purged of sin beyond the Day of Judgement. In the same way that the upper terraces of the Cardinal's garden are elevated and bounded by the Line of a Hundred Fountains, the model of the golden age of antique Rome is raised on a platform defined by ten fountain jets. The Cardinal's erudition and virtue was to parallel the culture of antique Rome.

Finally, the Rometta lies at the heart of a sequence of fountains which, under Minerva's influence, begins with the Fountain of the Owls: in the same way that the Venus sequence on the eastern side of the garden culminates in the Grotto of Venus relating to the secret garden, so the Minerva sequence culminates in a grotto above the horizon of the sibyl's journey – the Grotto of Diana.

FROM LEFT TO RIGHT: Cartari, Minerva. As the personification of the 'intellectual virtue of the soul', Minerva is born out of the head of Jupiter (left). She has a gilded helmet and crystal shield; Cartari, Venus. The carriage of Venus is pulled by two doves and two swans, birds sacred to her. She is crowned in myrtle, and on her chest she has the symbol of a burning flame. In her left hand she carries three golden apples, and in her right, a ball 'in the shape of the world'. She is accompanied by her handmaidens, three Graces who represent the three phases of love – beauty, desire and fulfilment. Alternatively, they are personifications of chastity, beauty and love; OVERLEAF: Rometta detail

The Grotto of Diana

One of the most pronounced errors in the Du Pérac engraving is the location of the Grotto of Diana, which is shown as being part of the Rometta. The cross-shaped grotto is in fact far removed, located high above the Rometta at the western end of the Cardinal's walk. There are two arched entrances into the grotto; one from the Cardinal's walk, and the other from a terrace to the west which also gives onto a spiral staircase to the outdoor dining loggia above. The crossing is marked by a much-altered, shallow vault which is decorated by a complex mosaic relief focusing on the Cardinal's coat of arms, entwined with apple-laden branches.

The principal entrance leads from the garden, and is flanked on either side by a small niche set into a panelled wall worked in mosaic. The niche to the right housed a statue of Penthesilea, the Amazon queen who came to the aid of Priam in the Trojan war. One of the labours of Hercules was to obtain the girdle of another Amazon queen, Hippolyta, for the daughter of Eurystheus. The Amazons venerated Diana, and some chroniclers attribute to them the foundation of Ephesus and the construction of the Temple of Diana. In the niche to the left of the entrance was a marble statue of the Roman heroine Lucretia, who was raped by the son of Tarquin the Proud. Putting herself and her family in terrible danger, she averted the authorities of what had happened and then took her own life. The ensuing rebellion led to the forced exile of Brutus and his family.

Opposite the entrance stood a white marble statue of the chaste goddess Diana with one of her hunting dogs. Diana's niche is worked in relief to allude to the walls of her sacred cave and is overlaid with a vine of white flowers. To the left is an illusionary opening which gives onto a sun-filled landscape, with Actaeon fleeing in the distance. The choice of this subject is perhaps surprising – it is one of the most violent associated with Diana. Ovid's *Metamorphoses* relates the tale. When out hunting one day, Actaeon chanced upon Diana, as she and her nymphs bathed naked. Seeing the intruder, the nymphs gathered around their chaste goddess to protect her from the huntsman's gaze. As her bow was not to hand, Diana flung water in Actaeon's face: 'Now tell you saw me here naked without my clothes, if you can tell at all'. With that threat, Actaeon began to transform: 'antlers she raised from his dripping head, lengthened his neck, pointed his ears, transformed his hands to hooves, arms to long legs, and draped his body with a dappled hide'. Actaeon, his body now that of a stag, fled. Misfortune followed him, for he was spotted by his own hunting pack, chased down and finally devoured by his own dogs: 'And not until so many countless wounds had drained away his lifeblood was the wrath, it is said, of chaste Diana satisfied'.[79]

To the left of Diana, facing west towards the opening onto the terrace,

is a second niche which housed a marble statue of Minerva.[80] The walls to either side of her and those immediately adjacent to the terrace depict various legends in mosaic and stucco relief.

According to Del Re, the panel nearest to Minerva represented the myth of Pan and Syrinx, an Arcadian nymph (in its actual condition, possibly as a result of restoration, it appears to depict Minerva with the Muses). Syrinx was pursued by Pan until her flight was blocked by the river Ladon. To escape the god's amorous intentions, the chaste nymph (who revered Diana) begged her sisters, the water nymphs, to transform her, 'and when Pan thought he had captured her, he held instead only the tall marsh reeds'. Hearing the 'witching tones' of the wind blowing through the reeds, Pan waxed together pipes of different lengths and made the pipes bearing Syrinx's name, crying, 'You and I shall stay in unison'. It is said that Pan left the very first pipes in a grotto near Ephesus, and these served to test a maiden's virginity. A girl's purity would be announced by the melodious music of the pipes and the opening of the door to the cave. Alternatively, mournful sounds would be heard and the girl enclosed inside would disappear. The panel to the left of Minerva depicts the scene of Perseus and Andromeda. Perseus was the son of Jupiter and Danaë (who had been beguiled by Jupiter's transformation into a shower of golden rain). He slew the fearful Gorgon Medusa with the help of magical weapons furnished by Mercury and Minerva. Returning with the Gorgon's head, which he had rashly promised as a gift to the tyrant Polydectes, he spotted the beautiful maiden Andromeda, chained to a rock in the sea and menaced by a sea monster. He fell in love and offered to save her in return for her hand in marriage. Her onlooking father agreed, and Perseus, with the aid of his magic sword, had little trouble in slaying the beast.

To the right of the Diana niche, the panel represents the legend of another Arcadian nymph, Callisto, who was seduced by Jupiter (this time disguising himself as Diana). Callisto's secret was disclosed when she was forced to undress in front of the other nymphs in order to bathe: 'Begone,' cried Diana, seeing her pregnant shape, 'You shall not stain my stream'. Callisto is shown fleeing from Diana, who has set her dogs onto her. On the birth of the child, Arcas, Juno was thrown into fury: 'Strumpet, so it has come to this, that you gave birth, and published by that birth my injury and proved my Jupiter's disgrace'. She transformed poor Callisto into a bear. After years of misery, Jupiter transported them both to the sky; mother and son became the constellations, the Great and Little Bears.

On the opposite wall is the legend of Daphne and Apollo. Daphne (whose name in Greek means 'laurel') was the daughter of the river god Ladon and of the earth. Fleeing from the amorous advances of Apollo, she in desperation begged her father to transform her into a laurel tree. In consequence, the laurel became Apollo's favourite tree. Ovid emphasised its connection with the Temple of Augustus, as a symbol of triumph:'When joy shouts triumph and the Capitol welcomes the long procession, you shall stand beside Augustus' gates, sure sentinel on either side, guarding the oak between'.[81]

The meaning behind these scenes, all precisely chosen from Ovid's *Metamorphoses*, is complex, and perhaps its complete sense has been lost to us. The statue in the grotto is that of Diana of Aricia, and she is aligned with the Diana of Ephesus which originally stood in the Water Organ (and related to the Tiburtine Sibyl – Leucothea was first transformed into *Mater Matuta*, see p5). Diana was the saviour of the Cardinal's legendary ancestor, Ippolito, who as a youth fell from his horse and was torn apart. The goddess beseeched Aesculapius to restore his life, and he was duly resurrected. Diana took him back to her sanctuary in Aricia, on lake Nemi, a place from which horses were excluded. As a consequence, Ippolito was identified with the god Virbio, the companion of Diana and the hero to whom, according to Muret, the gardens were jointly dedicated.[82] Diana is principally a figure representing virtue and virginity, the chaste hunting goddess of the woods, and the scene depicting Actaeon is a violent reminder of her wrath, should her chastity be threatened.

Apollo is said to have gilded Diana's crescent moon as he gilded the sun; in all the frescoes of Diana in the villa she is shown with a crescent moon above her head, as '*la illumatrice della notte*'. According to Cartari, she was the same as the goddess Hecate, reflecting the light of the sun into the earth's shadowy depths:

Her virtue has strength not only in heaven, where she is called the moon, but also on the earth, where she is called Diana, and below in hell, where she is called Hecate and Proserpina, because she is believed to be there when she is hidden to us.

The chastity of Diana, as the moon, reflects the light of the heavens and represents the diffusion of virtue on earth. Her association with Apollo probably accounts for the choice of the scene of Daphne transforming into a laurel, a tree also sacred to Diana: an ancient belief held that if you slept with your head bound by branches of laurel, the truth would be revealed in dreams.

Like Daphne, Syrinx asked to be transformed in order to protect her virtue. Pan, '*Natura Operatrice*' and the 'universal god', was often equated with Jupiter. As such, he was represented as the sun, with his horns being the rays of sun and the moon, pointing towards the heavens. Cartari explained that this could be interpreted in two ways: as representing, first, the art of measuring the stars, and second, the effects that the movement of the stars have on the earth.

Like Diana, Pan was identified with the heavens and the stars, and was a symbol of the effects of the planets on earth – a theme linked to the fleeing Callisto, who was saved when Jupiter transformed her into the Great Bear. Pan's great gift was his invention of the Syrinx, 'the representation of celestial harmony which, it has been noticed, has seven notes and seven different voices, like the seven heavens (*cieli*)'.[83] The musical Pan was associated with Minerva, as 'inventor of all the arts', an inventiveness also shown by the other panel flanking her niche, in which Perseus receives his magical gifts. On either side of Minerva's niche is a frieze of apple-tree branches. The most obvious allusion is to the apples of the Garden of the Hesperides, which Hercules had to obtain. But this is only part of the story, for the apples shown around the grotto, garden and villa are consistently five in number, not three, as is traditionally the case in the legends of Hercules. Other groupings of decorative elements are arranged in nines, like the motifs which frame Diana's niche (and like the birds in the frescoes inside the villa). This numeration must be a subtle allegory for the sibyl's prophecy of nine generations, the fifth being the generation following the crucifixion of Christ.[84] The scene of Actaeon, the focus of the grotto, is itself a crucifixion type and it is framed by a cycle of images relating to the theme of salvation which finally unites the grottoes imagery: Daphne, Syrinx, Callisto and Andromeda were all rescued from peril.

The materials of the grotto are reflective or transparent; fragments of clear crystal (one of Minerva's attributes was a crystal sceptre), glazed ceramic, semiprecious stones, coloured glass, flint and marble. The floor was also made entirely of ceramic. Immersed in water, the grotto must have been awash with sunlight; a sacred grotto dedicated to divine virtue as it is mediated on earth through wisdom, chastity and love.

PAGE 95: Cartari, Diana as the moon is shown with three heads, one of a horse (swift passage of the moon across the skies), the second of a dog (when it is not visible, the moon, like the dog Cerberus, is given to the gods of the underworld), and the third of a wild boar (related to Diana as it never leaves the woods). On the right, a white figure with the head of a sparrowhawk (consecrated to the sun) represents the reflected light of the moon; PAGES 96-97: Grotto of Diana, detail of ceramic floor; ABOVE: Grotto of Diana, Niche of Diana with scene of Actaeon

Grotto of Diana, Chase of Callisto

PAGES 100-101: Grotto of Diana, detail of ceramic floor; ABOVE: Grotto of Diana, Daphne and Apollo

Grotto of Diana. According to Del Re, this panel originally represented Pan and Syrinx. Possibly as a result of subsequent restoration, the scene now appears to depict Minerva with the Muses

The Salotto

The interior of the villa has no consistent iconographic structure, but rather was painted in groups of rooms by artists led by Girolamo Muziano, Federico Zuccaro, Livio Agresti and Cesare Nebbia over a period from 1565 to 1572.[85] Of these rooms, the Salotto, which is directly below the level of the Cardinal's apartments, particularly helps to illuminate the themes so far identified in the garden. And, along with several external rooms in the garden, the Salotto would have been the setting for the vastly elaborate banquets which were central to the life of the court.

These banquets, recounted in detail in the treatises of Giovan Francesco Colle and Cristoforo di Messisburgo,[86] were organised in accordance with a highly refined iconographic structure, which involved not only a transformation of the setting itself, to match a specific theme, but the invention of a highly imaginative sequence of dishes, costumes, table decorations and performances. The banquet of Giovan Battista Rossetti, for instance, lasted several days in a room redecorated to resemble a Temple of Neptune: the soffit was painted with waves and lit to form shadows in the shapes of marine creatures; the tablecloth was painted like the sea and populated by sugar sea monsters, rocks and serviettes which resembled fish scales and plates in the form of shells. A similar scene was described by Ligorio in his account of Domitian's 'infernal dinner' in rooms deep below the earth:

> One by one, the invited Senators were led down into the prepared rooms and were taken by evil spirits to be painted and undressed; they were then led to the dark place of the dinner and were seated with a black candle in their hands on a black stool upon which was written the name of each Senator dining with the infernal gods. When they were all painted, undressed and seated at the table with food and black plates, tablecloths and napkins, they were served by black men. At the top of the table was Domitian. During the dinner he spoke relentlessly of pain and torment, of murders and tragedies, of courageous and strange deaths, of the opening of chests and the ripping out of hearts with such speed that the victims held them in their hands while still beating. With these harsh tales, time passed . . . Finally, when the sad dinner was over, he sent them away through the opposite side of the room and they were filled with horror, believing that they were being led to their doom. Several white men appeared; they were washed, perfumed and dressed in new tunics and Senatorial togas, and were then led to the light to return home.

In Messisburgo's account, the emphasis shifts from a strict adherence to recipes and codified instructions towards a celebration of the spectacular nature of the banquet, with inventions, illusions and perspectival effects: 'the banquet which I created,' wrote Messisburgo, 'was all shadows, dreams, illusions, metaphor and allegory'. The accent was on the marvellous, artificial nature of the event: there are descriptions of Estense banquets with tables adorned by silver-winged peacocks with the feet and beak of an eagle, trees of salami, and every kind of fantasy in sugar and cake. Often a group of locals would be invited to attend: these banquets in the artificial settings of the villa tended to replace traditional calendar feasts and they would be related more to personal events within the noble family than celebrations affecting the community as a whole. The relation to theatre is obvious; the Salotto, Rometta and the Oval Fountain were all theatre-like in that they visually brought together cultural and historical themes and no doubt actual theatre in the event of a banquet.

At the lower level of the Salotto, the walls are painted with fictive windows and doors, which alternate with pairs of spiral columns to form the illusion of niches looking out onto a painted landscape. Above an elaborate stucco cornice is a curved white soffit, articulated with Grotesque figures and marked by pairs of deities in each corner around the Cardinal's impresa, and by a stucco relief at the centre of each wall. Finally, the middle of the ceiling is painted with an accelerated perspective which opens onto a scene of the gods feasting, with Jupiter and Juno at the centre. In this way, the illusionary architecture of the soffit structures the distance between heaven and earth; between the sacred banquet and the banquet in the room itself.

At the lower level, the corners of the two shorter sides have oval niches, which originally housed the busts of the emperors Helius Pertinax, Lucius Cornelius Sulla, Lucilla, daughter of Marcus Aurelius, and Gaius Julius Caesar. As with the topography of the garden itself, a dialogue is established between the iconographic themes of the Salotto and the history embodied in the Cardinal's collection of antique sculptures and archaeological finds. The ceiling perspective brings into focus the sacred feast, while the depth of the walls at the lower level alludes to a temporal distance; 'bringing to life' the honourable past, in Ligorio's words. The actual wall of the room is broken down to appear like a loggia whose perspectival openings draw the distant landscape, part-real, part-fictive, into the space.

Set in the centre of the northeast wall is a small fountain which is particularly important to the iconography of the room. Its exquisite mosaic panel represents a composite view of ancient Tivoli, with the Temple of Sibyl, the tower of the Tiburtine Cathedral (Temple of Hercules Saxanus) and, in a mosaic of black glass, the Grotto of Neptune or Sirene. This mosaic is a collage of the Tiburtine antiquities used to locate the garden's fountains, and is oriented towards the Muziano fresco of the garden on the opposite wall.

Originally, below the mosaic, until recently, stood a figure of 'Senta Fauna', a Tiburtine oracle otherwise known as Fatua or Bona Dea, whose origin was either by the lakes of the Acqua Albula or by the place where the waters flow into the Anio. The statue in the Salotto was black except for its feet, face and marble cornucopia-bearing hands, which were white. Boccaccio, citing Marcrobius, describes this deity as being the cause of all good, as she who feeds the products of the earth. She is identified with the nymph Albunea, who became a sibyl when the sibylline cults arrived at Latium. As *Mater Matuta*, Albunea was otherwise known as the Tiburtine Sibyl; her attributes resembled those of the Bona Dea, but she was associated with the water of the Aniene. Bona Dea, on the other hand, specifically belongs to the Acqua Albula and, as described by Del Re, to the water of the Rivellese, which feeds the fountains of the garden south of the Line of a Hundred Fountains. In addition, there were statues of Pan and satyrs. Cartari stated that Pan represented 'the sun, father of all things', and illustrated this notion with an image of a seated Jupiter and a standing Pan. He explained that, together, they represent the universe:

> The image of Jupiter and Pan signifies the Universe, one the god of the skies and the other the god of the pastures: the former, seated, signifies the immutability of god, his providence, and the other, in the midst of the world, stands and is shown moving.[87]

To allude to a genuine opening, the fountain is framed to resemble a real window, and to underline the subject of the scene, each of the two vertical panels are decorated with a band of nine garland motifs ending in a mosaic sun. The lintel of the false window frame has a delicate mosaic pattern comprising two sets of garlands around a bowl containing five apples in yellow mosaic. The window is flanked by two caryatids

supporting an elaborate cornice, on top of which are two branches holding three groups of five apples, intricately interwoven behind a white stuccoed eagle with a gilded beak. This repeated motif of five apples refers not only to the group of three golden apples from the Garden of the Hesperides (traditionally associated with the virtues of Hercules, whose statue stood on the Capitol), but to the generations of the world as foretold by the sibyl. The fifth generation, as the one following Christ's crucifixion, must represent his resurrection and ascension into heaven.[88] The window of the fountain niche frames a complex perspective of the distant Temple of the Sibyl in the context of the Tiburtine landscape; the setting of the room makes visible its relationship with the large perspective of the garden, covering the whole of the opposite wall. Between these two images, at the foot of Muziano's fresco, is an image of a white peacock, an ancient symbol of eternal life, which reflects the meaning of the repeated motif of fives (the apotheosis of Christ). The sibyl, as *Mater Matuta,* is then identified with Bona Dea (as goddess of Nature) and likened to Pan in her relationship to music. These images, together with the scene of the Feast of the Gods in the ceiling fresco, establish the Salotto as a representation of the Universe, of heaven and earth combined – like Cartari's image of Pan and Jupiter. The Salotto is like a visualisation of the Tiburtine landscape in its historical depth and in the presence of the gods.

The spatial structure of the curved soffit is ambiguous, and its iconography complex. A white ground is worked over a dark background which is revealed at the corners and in a band directly above the comice

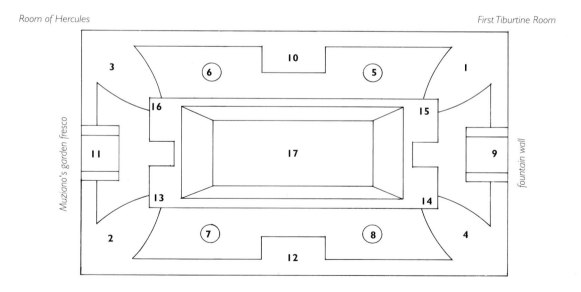

PAGES 104-105: Salotto, southeast wall; ABOVE: Salotto soffit plan drawn by David Dernie (1) Jupiter and Juno (2) Mars and Venus (3) Bacchus and Ceres (4) Mercury and Minerva (5) Jupiter with eagle (6) Juno in peacock-drawn chariot (7) Neptune in horse-drawn chariot (8) Pluto entering underworld (9) sacrifice to Diana (10) sacrifice of a goat to Bacchus (11) sacrifice of a pig to Ceres (12) sacrifice of a bull to Apollo (13) Spring (14) Summer (15) Autumn (16) Winter (17) Feast of the Gods

Salotto, northeast wall

Salotto, northeast wall detail

PAGES 110-11: The Salotto, soffit with Feast of the Gods; ABOVE: Salotto, southwest cove detail, Venus and Mars

level. Each of the walls has a scene of pagan sacrifice at its centre, framed in a Grotesque stuccowork, and in the middle of the resulting panels on the two longer walls is a small oval frame depicting Jupiter and Juno (towards the garden), Pluto and Neptune, together representing the dominions of the skies, earth and sea. As 'soul of the world', producer of all things, Jupiter's domain is decorated with the most exquisite Grotesques, a rhythm of transforming species which represents a generative nature in the room itself.

Ligorio described these transformations; like those in the cave of Proteus on the Caspian Sea, they represented the 'many things which make up nourishing, generative nature'[89], which he likened to the friendship between men. This *prima materia* (primary substance), Ligorio explained, touches the truth of ideas, and hides under the veil of 'poetic declaration' in the transformations of the Grotesque images. The ornaments could ultimately be justified on moral grounds:

> they are not formed by chance, nor for fantastical ends . . . they
> are made to create stupor and wonder, to show miserable
> mortals how much the fullness of the intellect and its imagina-
> tion can achieve and how it makes man erudite and expert in
> the sciences.[90]

In the corners of the soffit, paired gods surround the Cardinal's impresa, and above these, as part of the framing device for the ceiling perspective, are four small panels depicting the seasons. Spring, in the southwest corner of the room, corresponds to Venus, who is with Mars. Winter is related to Bacchus and Ceres (northwest corner), Autumn to Jupiter and Juno (northeast corner), and Summer to Mercury and Minerva (southeast corner).

It would be a mistake to consider this complex and precisely chosen iconographic programme in isolation from the garden, to which, as an illusionary loggia, it is so clearly related, both in the pictorial treatment of its walls, and in its setting as a partial cave, caught between an arbour-like passage (which links all the rooms of the villa) and the garden itself. In several ways, the Salotto refers to the iconography of the garden and, like the Rometta, also represents a synthesis of it.[91]

First the room, like the garden, is built out of explicit orientations to the surrounding landscape. These orientations are built into a vertical sequence which appears as part of the visual order of the room — and as a journey in the garden. Echoing the topography of the actual garden, the mosaic of the fountain niche in the Salotto is flanked by painted images of the Water Organ and Oval Fountain. Around this niche, the verticality of the room is articulated by the mediative architecture of the stucco-and-mosaic frame which cuts the cornice (in a similar way to the middle horizon of the garden), and forms the base to an image of a pagan sacrifice to Diana. Like the Grotto of Diana in the garden, which overlooks the Temple of the Sibyl on the southern edge of the Rometta, the panel representing Diana in the Salotto surmounts the mosaic of the Tiburtine landscape. The transition between the two levels of the room is further represented as a mediation of light reflected in the glass mosaic, which is patterned to refer to the sibyl's apocalyptic verses. These divinely inspired words bring forth light to the earth.

Second, the other deities represented in this domain of Jupiter are found at either end of the Line of a Hundred Fountains: Minerva, Bacchus and Venus. Bacchus and Venus are placed at the Oval Fountain, and Minervan iconography, as has been noted, stretches along the western edge of the garden between the Grotto of Diana and the Fountain of the Owls. This play across the length of the Salotto is analogous to the Line of a Hundred Fountains, and it is echoed below the cornice, between the fictive window towards the Temple of the Sibyl and the perspective of the garden, which extends towards the west and distant Rome.

Finally, at the centre of the ceiling, the room suddenly opens up with the accelerated perspective towards the heavens, where the dining in the room itself is reflected in the scene of the feasting gods. In the garden, the centre of the Line of a Hundred Fountains is broken by the tall jet of the Fountain of the Dragon, which was said to have been capable of reaching up to the level of the Cardinal's balcony. Full of fractured light, this symbolic jet touched the heavens, replaying the illusion of the Salotto fresco and completing the vision of the room as a visual summary of the journey through the garden.

The Line of a Hundred Fountains

The Line of a Hundred Fountains: Apotheosis at the End of Time

To return to the garden, the Line of a Hundred Fountains which symbolically links Tivoli and Rome is in a sense comparable to the length of the Salotto. The fountain is now so overgrown that it is impossible to see the original stucco panels representing scenes from Ovid's *Metamorphoses* (most likely on carved peperino stone), but it is nevertheless impressive as it stretches, unbroken, between the Oval Fountain and Rometta. It is a three-tiered structure which carries three water channels representing the three rivers flowing to Rome from Tivoli. In these waters, Ino was transformed into Leucothea and carried to the banks of the Tiber. The arrival at Rome of Leucothea, now in the role of the sibyl, is acknowledged by the miniature Campidoglio at the head of the fountain, and marked by a change of paving, from beaten earth to a stone that is similar to travertine, but softer and formed in sulphurous water.

The fountain is an unusual structure, for it completely closes the central axis of the garden and makes the Grotto of Hercules accessible only from above. Both Du Pérac's engraving and Muziano's Salotto fresco show a small flight of steps cutting the line of the fountain leading up to the niche of the reclining Hercules. The stair was not built; perhaps it was deliberately omitted to emphasise the boundary of the lower garden requiring the visitor to pass either to the Rometta or the Oval Fountain, or perhaps there was a practical problem which prevented its construction. Curzio Maccerone was preoccupied with work at Monte Cavallo, and did not arrive at the Villa D'Este until 1566. It is possible that a problem relating to the hydraulics was discovered at this relatively late date, for in the vicinity of the proposed staircase is a conflux of pipes, including the large feed to the tall jet of the Dragon Fountain (which required an enormous amount of pressure). The height of the Dragon jet was critical to the garden's meaning, and it could be that in order to resolve the details of the hydraulics, the central stair had to be sacrificed.[92]

Broken or unbroken, the Line of a Hundred Fountains serves a dual purpose. First, it articulates the relationship between the Oval Fountain and the Rometta and completes the legendary journey of the Tiburtine Sibyl between the Water Organ and the Rometta. Second, it creates a fundamental horizon in the garden. Above it, the garden takes on a strikingly different character: a sequence of diagonal paths work their way up the steep slope, culminating at the Fountain of Pandora at the level of the Cardinal's walk, which in turn gives onto staircases leading up to the villa and the adjacent secret garden. Below, the garden slopes gently down to an artificial plateau which was to be divided as a matrix of nine paths, as illustrated in Du Pérac's engraving. This arrangement is first of all a reference to the Apocalypse foretold by the Tiburtine Sibyl, and it underlines the role of the Hundred Fountains as an emblem of her journey between Rome and Tivoli. The representation of this theme comes together powerfully in the octagonal pavilion at the intersection of the cross-shaped arbour. From this space for contemplation, there would have been three views – ahead towards the Fountain of the Dragon, and to the east and west, towards the unbuilt fountains of Venus Cloacina and Neptune respectively.

Ahead, the glistening white marble statue of an enraged Jupiter served as a powerful reminder of the consequences of a wayward life. At his feet was the four-headed dragon, a symbol of the vanquished enemy of God, and above, the other two statues of Hercules, one in a dark niche showing him aged and reclining, and the other on the terrace above showing him holding Telephus, his son. Both statues would have been seen behind the light-filled jet of water which reached as though to the sky. Hercules, of course, stood as a symbol of redemption and was immortalised as a paradigm of virtuous life. In the villa itself, his perilous journey towards spiritual salvation is depicted in the Room of Hercules, and his reward, everlasting life in heaven, is depicted in the ceiling fresco of the Council of the Gods (see pp32-33).

If the central axis, the view straight ahead from the octagonal pavilion, was thus concerned with Salvation and Judgement at the end of time, then the transverse axis, extrapolated beyond the garden out to the Tiburtine Acropolis, was concerned with the Salvation of the Tiburtine Sibyl, who was saved by Neptune upon the request of Venus.[93] The image of the rainbow which was created over the pools reflects the rainbow which appeared to Noah after the Flood (Genesis 9, 12-16), and is a symbol of the union between heaven and earth and of the glory of God (Ezekiel 1, 28).

Just as the oak tree divides the Muziano fresco in the Salotto, this middle horizon between the fountain of Venus Cloacina and the Rometta bisects the garden, and represents a division of time and a passage into a world free of sin. Had it been built, the central staircase through the Line of a Hundred Fountains would have marked this transition from the fallen world to a time beyond the Day of Judgement, into a place announced by the presence of Hercules, whose apotheosis offered hope of salvation. This ascent would have completed the central drama of the whole garden.

Allowing for the width of the unbuilt stair, the number of metamorphoses panels on the Line of a Hundred Fountains approximates ninety, ordered in two ranges of forty-five. In the Salotto, the Grotto of Diana and the Rometta, emblems and materials also feature groups of five or nine, reflecting an ingenious combination of the two most important generations in the sibyl's apocalyptic vision – the ninth generation representing the Final Judgement, and the fifth generation following Christ's crucifixion and his resurrection into heaven. This final caprice clarifies the meaning of this central sequence: the life of Hercules can of

Line of a Hundred Fountains detail

course be paralleled with the life of Christ. Accordingly Jupiter, interpreted as God on his throne, sends down terrible rains on the Day of Atonement. An aged Hercules rests in his niche, like Christ entombed, while on the terrace above stands a youthful Hercules, resurrected, bathed in light and in a glistening jet of water, appearing to ascend into heaven. The Jupiter/Hercules/Christ sequence represents a clear Christian message of the love of God for the world, and the redemption of the world through Christ.[94]

Several references invariably come into play at every turn of the garden, which is structured as a cluster of room-like settings, each with a part of the story to tell. The overall character is one of openness, almost like a memory-theatre in which the full meaning is brought to light by the erudition of the observer. Each individual fountain provokes speculation on history and legend beyond the visible bounds of the garden, while the unity of the primary Christian message is clear, ingeniously unfolding as a journey through the garden.

The Christian reading of the garden is closely tied to the context of the Cardinal's position, the papal throne, the medieval monastery, and the devout personality of Ligorio. The explicit Christian iconography is understated. There are the twenty biblical scenes painted by Muziano in the entrance hall to the courtyard (see p119): here, Constantine, the first Christian Emperor, occupies the principal location over the Venus fountain. And in the villa itself, there is the Chapel and the Rooms of Noah and Moses (towards the secret garden), all painted before the death of Ippolito in 1572. In the secret garden is the Fountain of the Unicorn (a well-known allusion to Christ – as is the Fountain of Aesculapius in the main garden). In addition, the choice of Ovidian themes for the Grotto of Diana would seem to convey a Christian interpretation: the statue of Diana, as a symbol of the Trinity, is set in a niche with a mosaic depicting the tale of Actaeon (a crucifixion type). Finally, the Oval Fountain statue of the sibyl and Melicertes alludes to the Madonna and Child, an allusion undoubtedly picked up in an altar painting by De Vecchi in the church of S Eligio degli Orefici in Rome, in which the Madonna and Child sit at the foot of a cliff in the Tiburtine landscape with the Temple of the Sibyl in the background.

On arrival at the garden, the hope of redemption and everlasting life in heaven is presented as the apotheosis of Hercules, and as a transition between the thunderous darkness of the sins of the world to a spectacular celebration of light and sparkling water. The garden is then overlaid with a key horizon celebrating the Tiburtine Sibyl's divine gift of prophecy, marked by the unbuilt Fountain of Venus Cloacina,[95] the Water Organ, Oval Fountain and Rometta. The sibyl's journey between these fountains creates a path like a fragmented cornice around the fallen world below, and the garden – understood as a sacred room –

is structured around this horizon. Into it, like a fresco cycle, is built a sequence of fountains whose themes pertain to the sibyl. The sibyl legend is first referred to in Neptune and Venus, her initial saviours (she was saved a second time by Hercules). At the Water Organ she then appears as the goddess of nature in her Tiburtine cave; at the Oval Fountain she is likened to Mnemosyne, and finally, she is compared to Minerva who, in the guise of Roma, is placed in front of the Campidoglio at the Rometta.

The fountains can not only be read as an L-shaped journey across the garden, but can also be clustered in groups relating to Venus in the east and Minerva in the west. Like the tall jet of the Dragon Fountain, the sequence of these fountains implies a path between the lower and upper gardens. Venus is first uncovered, as Venus Cloacina, by taking the eastern arm of the cross-shaped arbour. On the path to the Oval Fountain she appears again in the Grotto of Venus, and for a third time in the villa itself, in the grotto oriented towards the secret garden. On the alternative path along the western arm of the arbour, Minerva appears first in the Fountain of the Owls, then again at the Rometta, and finally in the Grotto of Diana, as a crystal glistening in the western sunlight.

Human knowledge as a path to God is combined with Venus as a symbol of love, whose source is in the divine and whose impulse is the cause of natural and human creativity. It is this love, creativity and erudition which represent God's presence on earth. The artist cannot worship God artificially enough:'Disegno is the light of the intellect, nourishment and life of the sciences; another god created, another generative nature, a sun which drives and enhances every virtù.[96] And the mother of the Muses was the virtue of Mnemosyne (Memory), upon which, in Ligorio's words, the harmony of all things depends.

The journey through the garden then offers the visitor three principal choices. An eastern path tells of love as a sign of God's presence in the world (engaging the apse of S Pietro della Carità as a symbol of Christian love). To the west, the path reveals the virtue of the arts and human inventiveness oriented to admiration and contemplation of history – human knowledge and artistic genius demonstrate a closeness to the mind of God. Finally, along the central axis, is the symbol of a paradigmatic life of virtue, for which the reward is the release of the soul from the torment of the material world into heaven. All three paths ultimately converge on the Fountain of Pandora. The draped figure holds a vase which originally contained all ills. Devoured by curiosity, Pandora opened the vase, releasing all the ills over the earth. Only Hope remained inside. This hope of salvation at the end of time, marked by Pandora and combined with the Fountain of the Dragon, the Grottoes of Venus and the Minerva sequence, is the focus of the garden's meaning and the symbolic heart of the Tiburtine landscape.

Soffit to entrance to courtyard, Jacob Steals Isaac's Blessing

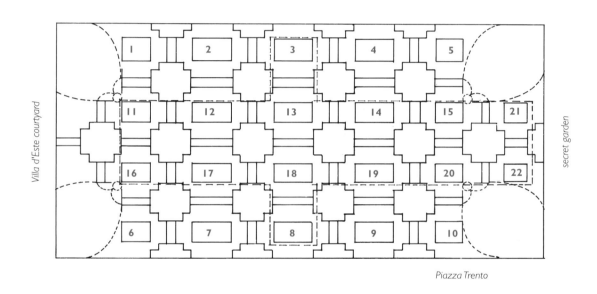

Villa d'Este courtyard

secret garden

Piazza Trento

Entrance hall to courtyard soffit, plan drawn by David Dernie (1) Genesis vi, vii, viii, The Universal Flood (2) Genesis iv v3, Cain Kills Abel (3) Genesis iii v6, Adam and Eve Banished From Paradise (4) Genesis XL, Joseph Interprets Dreams of Pharaoh's Eunuchs (5) Kings I xvii v9-23, Prophet Elijah and Zarephath (6) Genesis xxii v1-13, Abraham Sacrifices his Son to God (7) Genesis xxvii, Jacob Steals Isaac's Blessing (8) Genesis xxxvii, Joseph is Told of his Brother's Hatred (9) Judges xvi v16, Samson and Delilah (10) Damaged (11) Judges xv v15, Samson Kills 1,000 Philistines (12) Exodus xvi v15, Moses Feeds the Israelites (13) Genesis xxii v15-18, Abraham Blessed by the Lord (14) Genesis xxxix v7, Joseph and the Wife of Putiphar (15) Genesis xxi v9, Angel Comforts Hagar in the Desert (16) Numbers xxi v4, Moses and Bronze Serpent to Save Israel (17) Exodus iv v1, Moses' Branch Turned into a Serpent (18) Exodus xi v5, Moses and Aaron (19) Genesis xxxii v24-30, Jacob Wrestles with the Angel (20) Kings I xvii, David and Goliath. Above window to secret garden (21) 1 Samuel 16 v12 (Samuel's Annointment of David as King) (22) 1 Samuel 28 v7 (Saul and the Woman of Endor). The above are based on the Memorie Artistiche di Tivoli, Soprintendenza per i Beni Artistici e Storici di Roma, Rome, 1988. Some of the scenes are now invisible. There are several ways to interpret their structure, but one which is particularly persuasive is to acknowledge a pairing of particular scenes which creates the form of a cross over the entrance hall – much like the cross-shaped arbour which covered the entrance to the lower gardens. The length of the cross is formed from the following pairs: (11), (16) (Salvation by One); (12), (17) (God Provides); (14), (19) (Struggle With Faith Verified) (15), (20) (God's Strength) and (21), (22) (Wisdom of God's Choice of David). The transverse is made from (3), (13), (18) and (8) (Judgement of Sinners, Benediction of the Faithful, Salvation of the Children of Israel and Subsequent Reaction to Christ's Teaching – Joseph as Jesus type). Images (4), (9) and (2), (7) are paired (surrender of God's gift and conflict of brothers), and perhaps also refer to the sibyl (as interpreter of dreams), Hercules (Samson's Strength) and the Cardinal's conflicts with the Vatican. The images still visible at the four corners appear to allude to sacraments: (5) as anointment, (1) as baptism and (6) (as crucifixion type) as the Eucharist.

The figures on the following pages are drawings dated 30th April, 1565, which were found recently on the walls of the roof space above the reception salone on the piano nobile in the villa. The dragon above refers to the Cardinal's impresa and is accompanied by the phrase ab insomni non custodia dracone; *the dragon guarding the legendary Garden of the Hesperides was overcome by Hercules. It is represented as a cycle of waves – implying temporal and generative themes. These are particularly pertinent to the Fountain of the Dragon, whose oval form is depicted above. The oval is clearly constructed to contain three circles, as a symbol of the Holy Trinity. In this context, the dragon takes on the image of the vanquished enemy of God and its cyclical form refers to the cycle of death and resurrection of the fallen earth – as foretold by the Tiburtine Sibyl and as represented by the lower gardens*

The dragon in context. The date of 30th April 1565, indicates that the complex themes involved in the Fountain of the Dragon were conceived at an early stage. The phrase below, Io prospero fecit, refers not to Prospero, a person and possible creator of the garden, but to prospero, meaning prosperous (author's interpretation)

Nichel est Ovo. 'Ovo' *may refer to 'egg', although a translation as the 'egg/oval is nothing' makes little apparent sense. It would seem that a combination of alchemical themes and geometry is related to ideas concerning generative symbolism*

El Muro Biancho e Charta Del Matto. *The white wall is the wild card – a joker or perhaps zero in a tarot pack – which is able to travel between other cards. The white wall could refer simply to light, or to the white frescoed background for the Grotesque work (as a field which travels between their allegorical meaning), or more probably to the powerful double walls of the long corridor which linked all the rooms of the villa and is articulated with three fountain niches, like a garden wall*

Notes

1 See V Pacifici, Atti e Memorie della Società Tiburtina di Storia e d'Arte 1, 1921, p60, n1. Cited in D Coffin, The Villa d'Este at Tivoli, Princeton, New Jersey, 1960, p7.

2 See the manuscripts of Antonio Valle which are preserved in the Archivio di Stato in Rome and published in part in Memorie artistiche di Tivoli, Rome, p175 seq). He concludes that 'mentre maestro Bartolomeo dava di bianco al Palazzo, l'architetto Giovanni Alberto (Alberto Galvani di Ferrara) d'ordine del Cardinale si recava Tivoli per preparare tutto l'occorente per i lavori che stavano per cominciare. Il 22 del mese seguente egli tornava di nuovo e vi si tratteneva fino all'8 di novembre insieme a fra Giuglielmo del Piombo, cioè a Guglielmo della Porta che fu probabilmente l'ideatore del palazzo'.

3 See E Bourne, A Study of Tibur – Historical, Literary and Epigraphical – From the Earliest Times to the Close of the Roman Empire, Wisconsin, 1916.

4 See Il Libro dei Disegni di Pirro Ligorio, (ed) Caterina Volpi, Rome, 1994. Of Ligorio's frescoes only the Dance of Salome in the Oratorio of San Giovanni Decollato, Rome, survives.

5 P Ligorio, 'Trattato di alcune cose appartenente alla nobiltà delle'antiche arti . . .' in P Barocchi, 'Scritti d'Arte del Cinquecento', L'Artista vol vi, Turin, 1979, pp1448-50.

6 See T Comito, The Idea of the Garden in the Renaissance, Hassocks, 1979, p162, seq.

7 For a history of the villa see the numerous articles in Atti e Memorie della Società Tiburtina di Storia e d'Arte; FS Seni, La Villa d'Este in Tivoli, Rome, 1902; T Ashby, 'The Villa d'Este at Tivoli and the Collection of Classical Sculptures', Archaeologia xi, 1908, pp219-56; V Pacifici, Ippolito D'Este, Tivoli, 1920; D Coffin, The Villa d'Este at Tivoli, Princeton, New Jersey, 1960. Source material describing the work continued by Luigi d'Este (1572-86) the various Deans of the Sacred College, and finally Cardinal Alessandro d'Este (1605-21) includes: RW Lightbrown, Nicolas Audebert and the Villa d'Este, rewritten in its present form in 1582; Journal of the Warburg and Courtauld Institutes vol xxvii, 1964, pp164-90; U Foglietta, Opera Uberti Foglietae, Tyburtinum Hippolyti Cardinalis Ferrariensis, Rome, 1569; A Del Re, Dell'antichità Tiburtine, ch v, Rome, 1611; I Silvestre, Alcune vedute di giardini etc, Paris, 1646; F Croce, Delle Ville di Tivoli, Rome, 1664; L Moni, Villa Estense in Tivoli, Palestrina, 1702; G Venturini, Le Fontane del Giardino Estense in Tivoli, Rome, c1685; Fontaniere, Descrizione della Villa Estense di Tivoli, 1725; Ligorio, MS Barb. Lat. 5219, ff. 127-47: Descrittione della superba et magnificentissima Villa Tiburtina Hadriana di Pirro Ligorio dedicata all'Illmo et Rmo Sigre Hippolito Cardinale di Ferrara. See Archivio di Stato di Modena, file entitled Fabbrica et Ville, no 70, where most of the documentation (mostly accounts and contracts) referring to the Villa d'Este is kept.

8 The most obvious differences between the engraving and the garden are Du Pérac's inclusion of an additional lateral path between the Line of a Hundred Fountains and the terrace of the villa, the inclusion of the Fountain of Neptune (which, amongst others, was never built), and the position of the Grotto of Diana with respect to the Rometta. I argue below that the identification of Hercules in the central niche of the Fountain of the Dragon is incorrect.

9 See Le Antiche Rovine di Roma nei Disegni di Du Pérac, Florence, 1990.

10 Recall, for example, the enthusiasm with which Borromini described his Oratorio dei Filipini where, out of the knotted medieval street pattern, he achieved an ordered 'parallelogram without any imperfection', Opus Architectonicum, (ed) M De Benedictus De Riubeis, Rome, 1993, p32.

11 See the introduction to Ligorio's Libro delle Antichità in the State Archives in Turin.

12 Ligorio, Descrittione della superba et magnificentissima Villa Tiburtina Hadriana di Pirro Ligorio dedicata all'Illmo et Rmo Sigre Hippolito Cardinale di Ferrara, MS Barb. Lat. 5219, ff. 127-47.

13 This description is elaborated in Ligorio, Libro delle Antichità, Turin Cod. Ja II. J20. ff. 17r-20v. Ligorio described the circular temple as that of Vesta and the rectangular temple as that of Albunea. Under the voice of Albunea, however, he described the circular temple as that of the sibyl (see note 65), and locally the circular temple was always known as that of the sibyl (it is represented as such in the Second Tiburtine Room of the villa). For a description of the Villa of Augustus, see Ligorio, Villa di Augusto, Turin Cod. Ja II. J20. ff. 17r-20v. Quoted in full in Le Erme Tiburtine . . .,(ed) BP Venetucci, Rome, 1992, p180.

14 M Fagiolo, Natura e Artificio, Officina Edizioni, Rome, 1979, figs 85, 92. Fagiolo bases his interpretation on a seventeenth-century map of the region which aligns the Oval Fountain with the Temple of the Sibyl on the Tiburtine Acropolis. This map is inaccurate and I have used a modern map to illustrate my findings since the techniques for achieving precise alignments across a landscape were well known in the sixteenth century.

15 See Le Erme Tiburtine, op cit (note 13), pp179-81.

16 The Casino was begun under Pope Paul IV Carafa (1555-59) and completed by Pius IV Medici (1559-65). See G Smith, The Casino of Pius IV, Princeton, New Jersey, 1977, and M Fagiolo and ML Madonna, 'La Casina di Pio IV in Vaticano. Pirro Ligorio e l'architettura come gerolifico', Storia dell'arte xv/xvi, 1972, p237.

17 At an urban level, Pope Sixtus V (1585-90) undertook a massive restructuring of Rome, creating a sequence of visually structured links across the town related to liturgical processions between the major basilicas. See Roma Sisto Quinto, catalogue to an exhibition at the Palazzo Venezia, Rome, 1993.

18 Ligorio, MS Naples XIII. B. 9, in the State Archives in Turin.

19 Note, for example, Salviati's dining room in Palazzo Sacchetti, Rome. The black background which dominates this masterpiece is never lost, and creates a room where the iconography (principally the story of David) is underscored by the implicit presence of nature's creative impulse reified as its opposite. In the field of painting, Sebastiano del Piombo, for instance, tended to create a shadowy underpainting which swims beneath the transparent glazes of the surface colours. An image which perhaps captures this point is the frescoed cornices of fruit in Federico Zuccaro's map room at Caprarola. These are simply painted in black and modulated in transparent zinc white so that the darkness is never lost. What was always part of the implicit build-up of the depth of the image in the early Renaissance was now laid bare to reveal the fruits moulded out of darkness.

20 See Coffin, op cit (note 1), p79, who offers the translation 'the apples are no longer guarded by the sleepless dragon'.

21 Ibid, p85.

22 The Diary of Montaigne's Journey to Italy 1580-81, (trans) EJ Trenchmann, London, 1929, p167.

23 Despite Muret's dedication of the garden to Hercules, Foglietta, a personal

friend of Ligorio, failed to refer to Hercules at all in his description of the garden, and Ligorio himself seems not to have overelaborated the importance of Hercules – only on one occasion does he refer to the rectangular temple on the Tiburtine Acropolis as that of Hercules, and he identifies the gigantic temple just to the north of the garden not as the Temple of Hercules Victor but as the Villa Augustus (even though its true identity was known in the sixteenth century).

24 See Seni, op cit (note 7), p76.

25 The Hesperides were daughters of the evening and their garden lay on the west slopes of Mount Atlas. It contained the golden apples which Hercules was to recover as one of his feats for Eurystheus. Usually depictions of this legend show Hercules slaying the dragon but in this case he may have been omitted to allow a more specific allusion to the dragon as a device of the new Pope, Gregory XIII. The question which remains, of course, is whether this replaced an earlier arrangement in which Hercules was featured centrally, but this would seem not to be the case. The inventory of 1572 (when the fountain was largely incomplete) lists (no 9) 'A statue called Jove; the hands are wanting' at the entrance to the garden – presumably in this location until the Fountain of the Dragon was sufficiently complete.

26 Del Re refers to four nude male statues. One of these, a boxer, is mentioned by Zappi. It could possibly be the Castor of the inventory of 1572, no 31. The account of the Fontaniere calls it a valuable statue of a fighting gladiator; the inventories of 1752-53, published by Seni, refer to 'tre liberati pileati'. See Ashby, op cit (note 7), p253, footnote a.

27 Libro di M Pyrrho Ligorio Napolitano, delle antichità di Roma, nel quale si tratta de' Circi, Theatri, & Anfitheatri, Venice, 1553, p12. The oval form, the circumscribing path and the orientation of the central axis almost recreate the Tiburtine amphitheatre at the heart of the garden. The allusion to Rome's principal circus relates to the ancient rivalry between Tivoli and Rome and suggests that Villa d'Este itself is like the Palace of Tiberius, which overlooks the Circus Maximus from the Palatine Hill.

28 Both Zappi and the Parisian manuscript locate Leda in the central niche with Helena to her right and Clytemnestra to her left, and outside the fountain statues of Castor and Pollux, referring to the theme of Virtue and Vice. See Coffin, op cit, p81. On the central axis on the steep slope of the garden there were two other fountain niches (not three as shown in the Du Pérac). Immediately above the Fountain of the Dragon a niche housed a recumbent Hercules; on the terrace above was a further statue of Hercules standing with Telephus and a stag. The niche below the terrace at the foot of the facade to the villa housed three statues, Ione, Minerva and Pandora (who Audebert probably misidentifies as Psyche).

29 Vincenzo Cartari, Le Imagini De i Dei De Gli Antichi Nelle Quali Si Contegono Gl'Idoli, Riti, Ceremonie & Altre Cose Appartenenti Alla Religione De Gli Antichi, Venice, 1571, p130.

30 Orpheus recounted that Jupiter was the first and ultimate of all things, 'La Terra, L'Acqua, L'Aria & il fuoco, il giorno, e la notte, lo dipinge in forma di tutto il mondo facendo, che'l capo con la dorata chioma sia il lucido Cielo, ornato di risplendenti stelle, dal quale si veggono due corna uscire parimente dorate, che significano l'uno l'Oriente, l'altro l'Occidente, gli occhi sono il Sole, e la Luna, l'aria il largo petto, e gli homeri spatiosi, li quali hanno due grandi ali per la velocità de i venti, e perche Iddio si fa prestissimo à tutte le cose, l'ampio ventre è la gran terra cinta dalle acque del mare, i piedi sono la più bassa parte del mondo, la quale fanno essere nel centro della terra'.

31 See E Panofsky, Studies in Iconology, Humanist Themes in the Art of the Renaissance, London, 1972, p136 seq.

32 Cartari, op cit (note 29), p32.

33 Ligorio, 'Trattato di alcune cose appartenente alla Nobilità dell'Antiche Arti . . .', in L'Artista, Scritti del Cinquecento vol vil, (ed) P Barocchi, Turin, 1979, p1412-70. Cited in M Fagiolo, 'Il significato dell'Acqua e la Dialettica del Giardino: Pirro Ligorio e la Filosofia della Villa Cinquecentesca in Il Giardino Storico Italiano Problemi di Indagine Fonti Letterarie e Storiche' in Olschki, Il Giardino Storico Italiano, Problemi di Indagine Fonti Letterarie e Storiche, Florence, 1981, p199.

34 C Bartoli, Ragionamenti accademici sopra alcuni luoghi difficili di Dante, Venice, 1567, pp18-21 (quoted in Fagiolo, op cit, p199).

35 Ovid, Metamorphoses Bk 1, (trans) AD Melville, Oxford, 1986, p381 seq.

36 See R Jones, Tatti Studies vol 2, 1987, pp71-90; 'The Martyrdom of St Sebastian', 1460. In the upper left-hand corner is an image of a cloud containing a horseman which is 'not in the clouds but consists of a cloud' (Panofsky, Idea, A Concept in Art Theory, Columbia, 1968, p65).

37 Note the emergence of botanic studies during the sixteenth century as a science. Of particular importance is the treatise of the doctor and humanist Conrad Gesner, Historiae Animalium (1551-58), and the work of Ulisse Aldovrandi, whose first volume of Ornithologia was published as early as 1559. Ferrante Imperato's well-known Historia Naturale was published in 1599. For the collection of botanic works in the Estense collection see Immagine e Natura L'Immagine naturalistica nei codici e libri . . ., Modena, 1984.

38 In contrast to the tartaro, the two pilasters which frame Jupiter's niche were stuccoed and painted ochre. In addition two types of small ceramic tile were used to frame pairs of stucco pilasters. One appears like a yellow sun – like a lily on a deep blue background – and makes the illusion to the Cardinal's emblem of the fleur-du-lys. The second tile appears only around the Jupiter niche and figures a pair of yellow apples on a white background referring in part to the golden apples of the Garden of the Hesperides.

39 Cartari, op cit (note 29), p256.

40 Del Re casts some doubt on the view that the pieces of stone now at the western end of the pools belong to the unfinished Neptune: 'E nella nicchia di mezo del sopportico è destinata la statua di Nettuno dio del mare fatto da'Gentili, cominciata, e non finita, di molta grandezza, di cui si veggono la parte della testa, & altri membri in terra appresso l'ultima peschiere verso Ponente nel giardino secondo alcuni'. Del Re, op cit (note 7), ch v, part I, p69.

41 Cartari, op cit (note 29), p255.

42 According to Zappi, this bay is separated from the labyrinths by a wood of elm trees and is constructed as a loggia.

43 Ligorio, MS Barb. Lat., op cit, 'Questo appena entrato nella Città altamente dirpandosi, fà sentire lo strepito horribli del suo precipitio, & variamente diramadosi viene parte da una profonda voragine asorbito, che india poco dalla terra vomitato, corre ad inaffiare li campi Tiburtini.'.

44 See Le Erme Tiburtine . . . (ed) BP Venetucci, p180, Rome, 1992, vol 1, pp147-49. This villa is described by Ligorio in Turin, Archivo di Stato, Cod. Ja II. 7 J.20 ff. 11ss. It is now known as the Villa Gregoriana.

45 Lorenzo Moni Luccehese, La Villa Estense in Tivoli, Palestrina, 1702.

46 Montaigne, op cit (note 22), p166.

47 Zappi, Annali e Memorie di Tivoli, Tivoli, 1920, p42. Here Zappi describes the Temple of the Sibyl as 'sopra certe caverne sopra il pellago, circola di fori con il portico intorno di ordine corinto, fatto di pietre tiburtine stuccate fatte con ogni vera industria et artificio, lo qual tempio si ritrova fora dalle mura delle città, et

soprasta alla gran cascata del Pellago et anchi sopra la gran valle dello Inferno, ove si sommerge l'acqua, la qual casca con tanta grande violenza che produce il fiume verde'.

48 A Penna, 'La Sibilla Tiburtina e le Nove Età del Mondo', *Atti e Memorie della Società Tiburtina di Storia e d'Arte*, 45, 1972, pp7-95.

49 Saint Augustine's account in the 'City of God', bk 18, chp 23, coincidentally, has twenty-seven verses of the 'Erythraean Sibyl', or as others prefer to believe,'Cumean Sibyl'.The first letter of each verse makes up the words 'Iesous Chreistos Theou Uios Soter' which means 'Jesus Christ, the Son of God, the Saviour'. Further, if you combine the initial letters they make 'ichthys', meaning fish:*'Ligorio voce "Albunea" è nome di fonte et di montagna et di selva: ove era il Fano d'Albunea Sibylla Tiburtina. Eglino sono Via Valeria Tiburtina Plautia et le acqua del fonte cadeno nel fiume Aniene che hor si dice Teverone. Et dicesi Albuneo Fonte mascolinamente et nasce dall'Albuneo Bosco, chiamati dal l'oraculi et risponsi, che vi si davono da Albuneo Dea che i Greci chiamano Leucothea, et altramente detta da Latini Matre Matuta, et Albunea Sibylla come dicono il Fonte, lo quale è chiarissimo et nasci su una montagna, ove era l'oracolo della Dea: che fu una Sibylla nata presso de Thebani, et fu detta da essi Ino ... dal capo bianco, che ella passò fuggendo l'ira et furor d'indi in Italia, fu venerata per la Sibylla Tiburtina per che per le future cose ch'ella prediceva, ne fu adorata per una Dea, et gli fu conservato il Boscho, o Nemore Albuneo, et in Tibure gli fu fatto il Tempio circulare dell'ordine corinthio di sasso tiburtino, et d'essa parla Virgilio nel VII del l'Aeneide:'Lucosque sub alta\ consulit Albunea, nemorum quae maxima sacro\ fonte sonat', per che egli cade dal monte, et fa suono appresso dove haveva il suo Delubro, et chiamasi insino ad hoggidì Albunea Fonte'.*

50 Mercury is, of course, usually accompanied by Minerva. Is this legend included to reiterate the correspondence already made in the garden between Minerva (inventor of the arts), Mnemosyne (mother of the arts) and the Tiburtine Sibyl?

51 *See* Montaigne, op cit, p166 and GB Della Porta, *I tre libri de'spirituali*, 1601, n 8, pp85-86. Quoted in *Organi e Automi Musicali Idraulici di Villa d'Este a Tivoli in L'Organo Rivista di Cultura Organarica e Organistica*, Dec/Jan, 1986, p25. Aleotti's fourth theory was entitled *'Fabbricare una stanza nella quale al tempo che piacerà sempre vi spiri il vento, che la rinfreschi, e poco, e molto à volgia nostra'.*The system required two sealed tanks below the room to be vented. The villa is built directly over a Roman villa and between the two structures is an interstitial space, ideal for constructing such vessels. Francesco Caretta of the Villa d'Este drew my attention to a series of unusual pools of water at this basement level (some of which seem bottomless).

52 Quoted in Antonio Latanza, *The Hydraulic Organ in Music and Automata From Horology to Mechanical Instruments* vol 4, no 14, July 1990, p305. It was the first organ of its kind in sixteenth-century Italy, predating the famous automata of Pratolino – which was begun around 1569 for Francesco I de' Medici. Eugenio Battisti refers to evidence that Giovanni Fontana claimed the invention of the hydraulic fountain in 1425-32, although the first automatic musical instrument for which reliable data is preserved is that described by Banu Musa (a Baghdad scientific circle of the late ninth century).There were seven hydraulic organs in Italy: the Villa d'Este;Villa Pratolino, Florence (1569-80); Isola del Belvedere, Ferrara (destroyed 1599); Palazzo Quirinale, Rome (built in 1598 and rebuilt in 1647-48); Villa Aldobrandini, Frascati (1620); Royal Palace, Naples (1746), and Villa Pamphilli, Rome (1758-59).

53 The technique behind the Tivoli organ was later explained by Della Porta in his *Spiritali*. The method used by Erone was simplified and its use for au-

tomata, kilns and furnaces was outlined, noting in particular the ironworks, Ferriere di Nettuno, near Rome.

54 RW Lightbrown, Nicolas Audebert and the Villa d'Este (ms1576) in *Journal of the Warburg and Courtauld Institutes* vol xxvii, 1964, pp164-90, 180-87. Audebert arrived in Rome on the 6th October 1576 and left on the 2nd March 1577. My thanks to Alioune Sow for his translation of this text.

55 Audebert, op cit, p186. See also Zappi, op cit, p62.

56 The Du Pérac legend states that there were nine. Quoted in Coffin, op cit (note 1), p143.

57 Paris description, item 10; ibid, p145.

58 Note the curious circular structure which appears in several of the drawings of the garden by JH Fragonard (1760). *See* C Lamb, *Die Villa d'Este*, Munich, 1964, p150.

59 It is my assertion that the original cascade was both in the Grotto of the Sibyl itself and, as Del Re describes, in the niches of the upper facade.

60 Seni, op cit (note 7), Doc 4, 1609-12.

61 Ashby, op cit (note 7), Inventory 1572, item M – together with an eagle of travertine and a Goddess of Nature.

62 *See* Ovid, *Metamorphoses* Bk 4, v776-803, for a description of the birth of Pegasus from the blood of the Medusa's head, severed by Perseus.

63 *See* G Smith, op cit, p57, n6.

64 Ligorio, Naples, MS xiii B3, 64. Quoted in Smith, op cit, p41.

65 Ovid, op cit, Bk 5, v233-52.

66 *See* Cartari, op cit (note 29), p356.

67 The correspondence appears to be echoed in further detail. Among the dancing muses of the Casino loggia are two figures which Smith identifies as possible Bacchites.This would accord with the Oval Fountain, where the overflowing urn is addressed by two fountains dedicated to Bacchus.

68 Ligorio, Naples, MS xiii B. 3, 531. Quoted in Smith, op cit, p40, n44.

69 Ligorio, *Libro dell'Antichità Torino Archivio di Stato*, MS a. II. 14 J.27 (Diana Ephesia). Cited in M Fagiolo, *Il significato dell'Acqua e la dialettica del Giardino: Pirro Ligorio e la Filosofia della Villa Cinquecentesca,* in L Olschki, *Il Giardino Storico Italiano, Problemi di Indagine Fonti Letterarie e Storiche,* Florence, 1981, p204.

70 See note 31, Panofsky, op cit, p141.

71 Probably derived from Boccaccio: '*Esso Platone afferma essere tre soli amori . . . il primo de'quali disse esser divino, che si conface con la mente incorrotta, & con la ragione della virtù. Il secondo, passione di tralignato animo, & dimeni corrotta. Il terzo composto, overo per lo dilettevole; ma di declinante animo, & solamente per l'utile; meramente secondo l'openione di cicerone; lo chiameremo figliolo dell'Herebo, & della notte, cio è di cieca mente & di ostinato petto'.* G Boccaccio, *Geneologia degli Dei*, Venice, 1554, p18.

72 Del Re, op cit (note 7), p63.'*La piazza della Ciuetta l'ha tutta graffita dentro con fogliami, caccie di Metamorfisi d'Ouidio dentro, et fuori'. See also* Seni, *La Villa d'Este in Tivoli*, Rome, 1902, doc 4: 23.

73 Lucrezio, *(De rerum Natura), La Natura,* Milan, 1991, p3.

74 Ligorio, *Libro dell'Antiquità*, State Archives in turin, MS a. III. 11. J.9 'Homo'. Cited in M Fagiolo, *Pirro Ligorio et La Filosofia*, 1981, p200. According to the Du Pérac legend and Audebert, it was the Fountain of the Emperors.

75 Zuccaro, *L'idea de'Pittori, Scultori e Architetti del Cavalier Zuccaro*, Turin, Disserolio,1607, (ed) Detlef Heikamp, 1961, p170.

76 See *Il Giardino Storico Italiano Problemi di Indagine Fonti Letterarie e Storiche,* Florence, 1981. Maria Luisa Madonna, *Pirro Ligorio e Villa d'Este: La Scena di Roma e il Mistero della Sibilla*, Florence, 1981, pp173-96.

77 Del Re, op cit (note 7), p55.

78 Madonna relates the Rometta to a tradition of images where Rome is depicted as a single image. See *Nanni da Viterbo, Commentaria super opera diversorum auctorum de antiquitatibus loquentium confecta*, Rome, 1498. See *also* AP Fratz, *Le Piante di Roma*, Instituto di Studi Romani 1962, I, p64; II tav 33. During the nineteenth century the retaining wall collapsed, destroying most of the buildings.

79 Ovid, op cit (note 35).

80 The Du Pérac legend describes Hercules in this niche but in the 1572 Inventory, Zappi, Audebert and Del Re all identify Minerva.

81 Ovid, op cit (note 35), p383 n560ff.

82 Virbio is a play of two words 'Vir' (man), and 'Bis' (twice) – referring to the resurrection of the hero.

83 Cartari, op cit (note 29), p137.

84 The text *Ovid Moralisé* presents Christ's crucifixion as represented by the tale of Actaeon and Diana, whereby the moon's relation to the stars, their effect on the earth, and her relation to Hecate and the underworld, is interpreted as a symbol of the Trinity. This is flanked by two images associated with earthly delights: Pan and Syrinx, and the tale of Callisto – who is saved as she repents her sins. Opposite, Daphne represents the Virgin Mary and Perseus is a further Christ type as he saves Andromeda (as Eve). *See* C de Boer, *Ovid Moralisé*, Wiesbaden, 1966.

85 Coffin, op cit (note 1), p41 seq.

86 Barbara Di Pascale *Banchetti Estensi La spettacolarità del cibo alla corte di Ferrara nel Rinascimento*, Imola, 1995.

87 Cartari, op cit (note 29), p72.

88 *See* Coffin, op cit, p79.

89 Ligorio, *Grotesques*, p2676. For the myth of Proteus see Homer (Od 4 385ff).

90 Ligorio, *Grotesques*, op cit, p2671.

91 In a similar way, the quartered gardens around the pavilion can be interpreted as a room aligned through its centre with the Temple of the Sibyl (represented by the mosaic of the fountain in the Salotto), and with walls of planted espalier. The flowers of the northeastern section refer to Jupiter who is often shown with garlands of spring flowers whilst the cherries in the southwestern section are often a symbol of spring and therefore of Venus.

Bacchus is most commonly found in a garland of myrtle and thus is possibly referred to in the northwestern section. Finally, garlands of pine were given to Diana, whose grotto was shared with Minerva, which suggests that the set of lower gardens around the pavilion were intended as an analogue to the space of the Salotto. The direct line connecting the pavilion with the temple is framed by fir and pine, and the box *parterres* beyond. The passage in Isaiah, 'The fir tree, the pine tree and box together, to beautify the place of my sanctuary' (Sibyl's Temple), seems to describe the layout precisely (Isaiah 60:13).

92 It is also true that if the stair had gone ahead, it would, judging by the present levels, have been exceedingly steep. As a result of its omission there is an unresolved detail where the fountain terminates at each end.

93 Not only is the Fountain of the Sea the complement to the dark earth-like walls of the Dragon's cave but it embodies themes relating to death and the destruction of the world. It is the dark and mysterious domain of monsters and is described, like the Tiburtine Cascade, as hell. If ahead the Dragon Fountain structured a transformation, represented as a movement between dark and light (as water), the image of the vanquished enemy of God and the apotheosis of the virtuous spirit, then the Fountain of the Neptune, silhouetted against the western sunlight, was to represent infernal darkness and the fallen world – to be saved by Christ as he casts his net onto the sea, or by the Apostles as fishermen: the church itself is often depicted as a boat on the sea of the world.

94 In versions of *Ovid Moralisé* both Jupiter and Hercules are identified with Christ: *'Jupiter représente le Christe, qui descende vers Sidoine en Tyre, sur la terre, pour sauver l'humanité. Pour cela il se fit homme et souffrit, mort et passion pour nous'*. C de Boer, op cit (note 84). The hope of eternal life in heaven as the central message of the garden accounts for the image of the peacock, a symbol of eternity, in the foreground of Muziano's Salotto fresco.

95 Venus Cloacina appears in the Du Pérac legend and in Audebert's description of the garden. There was a temple to Venus Cloacina on the Roman forum, where she is related to the Cloaca Maxima. Her association with purification and divination most likely account for her presence and location at the Villa d'Este.

96 Zuccaro, op cit, p79.